MAKING CHURCH MUSIC WORK

MAKING CHURCH MUSIC WORK

by
LIONEL DAKERS

Director of the Royal School of Church Music

Addington Press

Series No. 1

MOWBRAYS
LONDON & OXFORD

© A. R. Mowbray & Co Ltd 1978

ISBN 0 264 66470 1

First published in 1978 by A. R. Mowbray & Co Ltd
Saint Thomas House, Becket Street, Oxford OX1 1EG

Phototypeset by Western Printing Services Ltd, Bristol
and Printed in Great Britain by

Lonsdale Universal Printing Ltd., Bath, Avon

INTERNATIONAL CHRISTIAN
GRADUATE UNIVERSITY

'. . . the letter killeth, but the spirit giveth life'

Contents

1. Stating the case   1
2. Interpretation   6
3. Making the printed page come to life   12
4. The influence of the organist as an accompanist   32
5. The influence of the conductor   39
6. How to choose the music   48
7. How to rehearse   57
8. Check list of anthems   153
    List of abbreviations   155
    Collection of anthems and motets   157

Stating the case

At the outset I must stress that this book is intended for those who we sometimes conveniently label the 'average' organist, choirmaster and conductor, many of whom genuinely wish to gain help and extend their expertise. It is not written for the cathedral organist, nor necessarily for the needs of those at major parish churches. Even so, I hope that much of what I have to say may be of some interest to musicians in these two categories. I also hope it may perhaps be read by some of those who *think* they know all the answers.

I would stress that it is essentially a practical book, for virtually every observation or suggestion springs either from personal experience or from those whose brains I have picked over the years.

In my work for the RSCM I see countless church musicians in action; the spectrum is an exceedingly broad one with the sum total an invaluable help in assessing the overall picture.

When planning out the shape of the book, I had hoped it might be possible to supplement my comments on the eighteen specific examples in Chapter 7 with a cassette. This would have provided an opportunity for the reader to hear for himself not only how certain passages should be treated but how they should *not* be treated. As this was not possible I have had to try to write down what would have been so much easier to explain and demonstrate on tape. I hope the reader will take this into account when studying this particular section of the book.

An alternative title might well have been Making Church Music Come to Life or, for that matter, making *any* music come to life. This is a fundamental truth on which all artistic effort should hinge, yet for some strange reason this sometimes presents a deficiency where church music is involved. It must be said that vitality and energy are not always commodities synonymous with the performance of music in church. Our forbears of a generation or more ago did not help matters by confusing these things with what they termed piousness. Nor did they stop at the music, for it was seen in other guises such as a religiosity and a misplaced interpretation of solemnity, features of a self-righteousness which did tend to mark out much of the Church in the nineteenth century.

Today we go straight to the heart of the matter and call it dullness. Even in our more enlightened days, joy and vitality are not commodities always in ready supply in church circles or, if they are there, they are sometimes indicative of a misapplied mateyness and a free-for-all which is equally as dangerous in its way.

As I go around the country—and for that matter the world—I do find a surfeit of church music which fails to come to life because, to use modern jargon, it fails to 'take off'. I see this so much that even if it sounds like a catalogue of condemnation, it is a tale which must be told. These sins of omission fall into a number of categories:

1   A lack of vision on the part of the choirmaster which is swiftly relayed to those on the receiving end.

2   Poor tuning, poor chording and poor blend. These underline the efforts of a choir not conditioned to a constant awareness of the over-riding need to listen. This

surely is a fundamental necessity of all music where the performers have to make their own notes. It applies no less to a singer than to a string player.

3 The lack of 'know how' seen in the failure of many a choirmaster to know instinctively what is wrong and, even more to the point, how to put matters right.

4 The inability to 'fire' a choir. This is frequently due to the numbness of the person in charge. A repetitive weekly routine can be contributory towards the unenthusiastic singing which swiftly results from this attitude of mind.

5 The music itself. Much of the less adventurous or safe repertoire found in many a church is conservative and one-track to a degree.

6 Everything sung in the same way and in the same style whether it be Byrd or Britten. There is no one uniform style in any branch of art. How much we miss out on when we iron out our music into a sameness and, in doing so, possibly relay what the composer never intended.

7 Choirmasters whose approach is in terms of the organ instead of vocal or choral techniques. This reflects the thinking of those who are organists first and foremost, and whose being a choirmaster is usually a sideline.

These are some of the negative aspects of the task and sometimes as much applicable to the professional as to the amateur. It is surely more to the point and certainly more constructive to come to terms with these shortcomings than to take false crumbs of comfort from those areas of activity where things are progressing happily and to good effect.

This all adds up to a catalogue which sounds, and is, dismal. This book sets out to provide a measure of propaganda aimed at combating the fact that *what is second rate elsewhere is often considered first rate in church music*. It is, moreover, a sad reflection that this state of affairs prevails in no other branch of musical endeavour. Maybe the plea of being amateur, a fact which anyhow encompasses the bulk of church music activity, is made the excuse for allowing inefficiency. How much better if we viewed the concept of professionalism as the pursuit of doing all things well instead of suggesting, even if by implication, that this is applicable only to the person who happens to earn his or her livelihood through music.

Because it proved impossible to illustrate my points through a cassette, I have had to be content with expressing my thoughts in words. This is not easy. As I see it, there are certain guidelines in this which repeatedly appear.

Grouped together they could be described as 'How to go about the task'. Broken down into constituents they include:

1 The influence of the choirmaster as seen through his skill and personality.

2 A choir consists of human beings, with all the limitations—and opportunities—this presents.

3 So much of choir training is common sense.

4 So much of choir training rests on all concerned using their ears 100 per cent.

5 The need for the choirmaster to be natural, which means being yourself and not putting on airs and graces, a balloon which will quickly be exploded.

6 The need for colour in all musical interpretation.

7 Every country in every generation reveals different styles, with different types of people conditioned by social circumstances. While appreciating this and, because the field is so wide, I have confined myself to English church music.

When all is said and done, a book such as this can only tell part of the story. In the end it is the personal experience, the contact, the actual doing which counts. I happen to be but one of many who would readily subscribe to having learned much through watching experienced choir trainers at work and, in doing so, picking up the tricks of the trade through a process of trial and error. What is more, at fifty plus I still find myself learning in this way.

Each choirmaster has his own approach and method to the task. This inevitably, and rightly, rubs off on a choir as it also will on any person observing and wishing to learn over a period of time. This is a process which works both ways but it does mean that a choir reflects its choirmaster, and this for better or for worse.

Certain things I shall say have been said before, some of them many times, by others as well as by me. The fact that these things need saying again and again serves to reinforce the need to reiterate fundamental truths as much as to fire warning shots where such are needed.

Human nature being what it is, we all too readily opt for the easy way out instead of pursuing the steep and rugged ascent we needs must take if integrity is to prevail. This, in terms of music, means that high standards must obtain. These standards, as we shall see, comprise many components of which correctness of notes is merely the basic point of departure.

It is through constant endeavour and unremitting hard work that the best in terms of performance will result, for hard work coupled with encouragement are the ultimate arbiters and both need to be dispensed in ample measure. The end product of such action applies at all levels of endeavour, given the right resources and the staying power.

In this respect I believe that the work of the RSCM can be of help and value through the facilities we provide for all areas of ability and for all who play any part in making worship through music the more real and complete.

2

Interpretation

INTRODUCTION

The particular quality of music versus the other arts

In the visual arts, such as painting and sculpture, the individual interprets with his eyes. How he interprets and is uplifted or otherwise in the process is a personal matter, a solo preoccupation between himself and the object he is looking at. In sculpture, and to a limited extent in painting, it is through the process of returning to a particular work again and again and viewing it perhaps from different angles and in different lights, that we interpret in a variety of ways, but always at our leisure and at our own time.

Not so music. In the first instance music, in company with theatre and ballet, relies heavily on movement—and ordered movement both physical or rhythmic, and in a time dimension. This brings to life, and through sound, what is otherwise a dead printed page. As an abstract form it does this through needing a third party, the performer, who in relation to composer and listener, is a go-between.

Nor does it stop there, for the performer interprets on his own terms. We, the listeners, have the double bonus of

6

hearing what the composer wrote, plus a personal interpretation of those sounds through attendant instrumental or vocal techniques.

In listening to music we therefore have, on balance, the best of a number of worlds involving an entire spread of resource ranging in church music from village to cathedral.

Even more unique is the fact that music is a moving art. The sounds are instantaneous for a particular and transitory moment in time. As such they can never be completely recaptured. In terms of a living performance the experience is a momentary one. In terms of a gramophone recording we can, and do, hear it repeated many times, but in this instance the repetition we hear is always the same interpretation, although our particular mood may cause us to be more moved by it on some occasions than on others.

In painting you can centre your eyes on a certain feature of the canvas and linger over it. Not so in music, for music relies on continuity for its validity and integrity. It moves from point A to point B as a continuous thread, with pulse and rhythm as essential factors in its scheme. It is created in a time dimension with the composer judging the distances to be encompassed.

Some have tried to break away from this restriction, but with little success or real conviction, merely because this goes against the entire ethos of what musical sound is all about. As music is by necessity conceived, shaped, and interpreted within a time structure it possesses a unique quality which, as such, singles it out from the visual arts. From this it is but a short step to something we have all experienced—the performance which lingers long in the memory as being head and shoulders above other performances. The reverse can also sometimes obtain.

So much then for the individual interpreter whom we choose to call the soloist. Where group activity is concerned, the individuals are in their turn dependant on each other and, for want of a better word, an overseer. Hence the choir trainer and the conductor. In ideal circumstances music is made to come alive through this particular person who influences and moulds his forces to subserviate their individuality as such, and to a certain extent their personality, in the cause of thinking and performing as an ensemble. In doing so they derive both an individual and a corporate satisfaction for themselves as well as for the listener.

In this type of performance no one person can be allowed to express a personal whim or fancy if it be at the expense of the whole. A blatant example of this is the obstreperous singer who persistently predominates. No less serious is the individual who underplays his or her appointed role.

What the choirmaster achieves in drawing the best out of his forces is done through his personality no less than through his skill as a musician and an interpreter reacting favourably on them. For this reason, no two performances are ever alike. This is one of the exciting—and frightening—aspects of music, which account for no less than twenty-nine different recordings of Beethoven's Fifth Symphony, to take but one random example.

Each performer is individually affected by personal mood. If you have had a row with the wife just before rehearsal and consequently arrive at church looking and feeling gruff, you are likely to coax a gruff sound from your choir. Weather can be another determining factor, with a bright and sunny day reacting much more favourably than will a wet and gloomy walk to church.

In a similar way, the mood which determines the inspiration of the conductor reacts strongly on the choir. Never underestimate the power you wield in this particular respect. At one time I did, and often, until my wife told me, wondered what was wrong with my singers and why they were frequently so unresponsive.

So much then hinges on the personality, the drive, the ability to communicate—call it what you will for it is all part of the same thing—which emanates from that one person, the choirmaster. This will reveal itself in him both as a person and, more particularly, as a musician who knows what choir training is all about and is prepared to persist until he gets the results he wants and for which, in the end, the choir will respect him the more.

All these, and other factors, add up not only to produce a performance in the real sense of what that means, but also satisfaction, enjoyment and stimulus as necessary ingredients. Music is the most social of artistic activities involving, in terms of the church choir, groups often widely varied in age, temperament and technical capabilities.

SOME GENERAL GUIDELINES

1. Beware of what looks easy on paper. It will probably be much more difficult than you bargain for in terms of a musically convincing interpretation. So much church music is predictably chordal, SATB orientated and moving in notes of equal value probably doubled up by the organ. Ouseley's *From the rising of the sun*, as but one example in this respect, has a marked similarity to many a hymn tune. What little rhythmic movement there is is almost identical with the hymn tune *Neander*, usually associated with *Come, ye faithful, raise the anthem*.

This type of music—and there is a great amount of it—is frequently labelled 'religious', which usually means serious and ponderance *in performance*. How often it is made to sound just that, while being equally dull and unrewarding for the listener.

Highly charged rhythms are sometimes construed as having secular leanings and therefore, for some unaccountable reasoning, not suitable for use in church. This can even be carried to the extent of being uncomfortably embarrassing for some. A mere glance at much church music down the ages, especially Viennese and Italian mass settings of the late seventeenth, eighteenth and nineteenth centuries, is extremely revealing in this respect, while the rhythmic complexities of some of the Flemish music of the fifteenth century and composers of today such as Penderewski and Charles Ives, make Britten's *Jubilate* seem quite tame by contrast.

A further factor is that for many of us contemporary 'light' music, frequently more rhythmic than melodic, is a constant and inescapable companion in restaurants, aircraft and through portable transistor radios. While this may be a comparatively new experience for some of us, the young of today are virtually weaned on such music. For them, much traditional church music must seem very dull, strange, and thoroughly alien.

2. In modern editions of Tudor church music, most barlines have been inserted editorially and mainly as a visual aid, music without fairly regular barring being awkward for many of us to follow. But, the melodic strands are the important factor even if they result, as will be seen in the anthem *Rejoice in the Lord alway*, in word stresses coming on any beat of the bar. In Tudor music we frequently have to think in such terms and not in the more familiar, and more modern, concept of regular barring which dictates an accented first beat.

3. In performing sixteenth- and seventeenth-century music we labour under certain illusions in that, consciously or not, we tend to interpret the music in the light of our musical experience during the intervening period between then and now. For example, it would perhaps be helpful if we could perform Byrd or Purcell as if we were living in the sixteenth or seventeenth centuries and consequently never knew of Brahms or Britten. The music which spans the period between then and now can so easily colour our faculties in an unreliable way.

4. This leads on to understanding the personalised style of a composer and how to interpret his music accordingly. Although this is an essentially basic point of departure it is

far too often glossed over in favour of a generalised and frequently inaccurate approach which bears little resemblance to any given style and which results in a whitewashed sameness of interpretation.

3

Making the printed page come to life

Long before interpretation can become a reality there *must* be basic accuracy of notes, both in pitch—which means tuning—and in timing. It follows that the choirmaster, in his role as choir trainer, must first be able to hear accurately what is wrong and then be able to put it right. Many choirmasters hear sounds which they vaguely recognise as incorrect. The choirmaster whose ear is unable to pinpoint a fault, say what is wrong, and then correct it, is at a disadvantage which will inevitably retard the work of his choir.

The ability to isolate faults, especially in the inner parts, is only an extension of the fundamental disciplines of aural training. It is confusing and singularly unhelpful to say to those on the receiving end, 'Will you sing that line again? It's not quite right.' A choir can only be expected to correct its mistakes, and learn from them, when they are clearly pointed out and the singers given some indication of *how* to correct them. This, surely, is teaching in its fullest sense.

The correctness of notes in music has its parallel in the bricks and mortar fundamental to the building of a house. Both are necessary construction materials. You can no

more produce satisfactory and artistic musical sounds
without basic accuracy and security than you can build a
house, however beautiful it may be to look at, without basic
building materials. Either will otherwise run the risk of
collapse.

THE BUILDING MATERIAL

What follows is dependent on a basic commodity, the ability to listen. This is a common point of departure as much
for the choir trainer as for the singer. *The singer is akin to
the string player in that both have to make their own notes*.
The ear, and the ear alone, determines the reliability of
pitch, whether the sound is made individually or as a group,
unison or harmony. Compare this with the keyboard player
whose notes are ready made.

First in order of priority, comes

PITCH

It is relatively easy to pitch single random notes with fair
accuracy, this despite the widely held belief that because a
child cannot immediately do this, he or she is automatically
tone deaf. All it probably means is that some training is
necessary. The incidence of total tone deafness is much
smaller than is frequently realised.

Intervals, which mean the gap between any two notes
more than a step apart, will present relatively few obstacles
if the particular and individual character of each is understood from the outset, can be heard in the mind, and then
sung accurately.

Each interval has its own distinctive personality.

Upward intervals are usually easier to negotiate than
downward ones. The major 7th is a good example of this,
bearing in mind that this interval is only a semitone less
than a full octave. It will help if we think of it as very slightly

less than an octave rather than what would seem to be a long haul up from the bottom note.

The universal tendency towards flatness in singing wide upwards intervals such as the major 6th and 7th is usually caused by thinking, even sliding, upwards by degrees, rather than by an energetic catapult which lands you directly on a bull's eye target, which is the centre of the note.

The second half of the ascending melodic minor scale and the first half of its descending form are helpful towards accuracy of the major and minor elements in the intervals of the 6th and 7th.

Correct tuning of major and minor 3rds is essential for any triad, chord or scale, the third being the note determining its tonality. Whereas the upward interval of a minor 3rd is unlikely to present many problems, the major 3rd, although only a semitone further, needs considerably more sharpening than is sometimes realised for the interval to have the brightness and vitality which is its essence.

In terms of aural perception it is so easy to confuse the perfect 4th with the perfect 5th. Great care must therefore be exercised in training the ear to recognise and reproduce these sounds. The anthem *Rejoice in the Lord alway* (page 66) is, as with so many examples of Tudor music, full of rising fourths.

The strength of the major 6th makes it a memorable sound when accurately tuned, the more so when the interval moves from a weak to a strong beat. Two good examples of this come at the opening of the hymn 'The day thou gavest, Lord, is ended' to the tune *St Clement* and the opening of Parry's fine tune *Laudate Dominum* ('O praise ye the Lord'). In both instances there must be an energetic spring upwards to the *top* of the interval, a relatively long-ish way.

Downward intervals generally need more practice than upward ones. A frequent tendency to flatten is probably due to a gravitational pull. Otherwise, identical care is needed with many of the points mentioned earlier being worked out in reverse.

Two further important points, the one linked with the other:

1 All accidentals, which are notes foreign to the key centre, must be carefully tuned and coloured. This without fail and in every instance.

2 Tones and semitones must similarly be tuned with equal care. A downward succession of semitones, especially if unaccompanied, as on the second page of John Rutter's *God be in my head* (see page 115) can, within a short space of time, contribute towards instability of pitch.
   It must always be remembered that a semitone is a very small interval.

If there are two or more vocal parts sounding at the same time, or if there is a harmonic accompaniment, the singers must feel the tonality and key centre. In this respect, listening to the other parts is so important and so helpful. In this way the singers can relate their line, and therefore their intervals, to other sounds. This using of harmonic context is a double check for accuracy.

The hearing of sounds in one's mind applies as equally to the singer as to the choir trainer whose task it is to co-ordinate individual sounds.

INTONATION

Whereas faulty intonation is accelerated through inaccurately measured intervals, out of tune singing can be the result of a number of factors, the most common of which are

1 Excitement, which produces sharpness.

2 Lethargy, or lack of ventilation, both of which produce flatness.

3 Looking unhappy. A long face with no sparkle in the eyes or hint of a smile, will also contribute towards flatness. It is a natural psychological reaction.

4 Personal mood, be it of elation or unhappiness, will each contribute in equal measure.

5 Weather plays a prominent part. While frost will help to brighten singing, mugginess and humidity will have the reverse effect.

If, in singing unaccompanied, a choir soon goes sharp or flat, the chances are that, for some inexplicable reason, once having shifted either way almost as if by an irresistible magnetic pull towards a new key centre, it will stay there.

Certain keys have a mood or character which is unhelpful in this respect. F major being generally found to be a particularly 'grey' key, it often helps to transpose up a semitone to the much brighter sound which F♯ offers. But always look first at the overall range of the individual lines; while transposing can help certain problems, it can have the reverse effect of making a line uncomfortably high or low.

The end of William Harris's anthem *Faire is the heaven* is a notorious example of a combination of all the difficulties discussed here. Maybe, having successfully negotiated ten difficult pages, singers tend to relax just before the end, only to find themselves confronted with the most difficult and demanding final bars.

NOTE LENGTHS

While a succession of notes of equal length are, or should be, easily negotiated, other matters can present pitfalls for the unwary. Time and rhythm can frequently play tricks on the unsuspecting performer.

Long notes are invariably given short value.

If, in counting equal notes, the normally accented beats are slightly, but rhythmically, emphasised, this will help to ensure full value:

1   2   3   4

In singing, a long final note needs careful negotiation. It is not always realised or understood that, for example, four beats last until the commencement of the fifth beat. The parallel here is in walking four miles, the fourth mile ending at the moment the fifth begins. Therefore a final consonant is sounded *on*, not before, the next beat:

4/4 | 1 2 3 4 | 1
    | Je - - - - | sus

For this reason, it is far more satisfactory if a pause, which is nebulous and can be interpreted at will, be given a specific and agreed number of beats.

Where a group of people are singing together, the need for unanimity is the more essential. It only needs one person to sound a final explosive consonant, such as an 's', in advance of everyone else, to produce the distraction we have all at some time experienced and which draws our attention away from the music as such.

Some composers, such as Vaughan Williams in his *Five Mystical Songs*, in writing ♩–♪ presumably meant the final 't' to sound on the quaver. This is another way of coming to terms with the same difficulty.

These principles apply even more to dotted notes where the tie must be firmly and rhythmically felt and never hurried.

♩.   ♪ ♩

1   2 AND 3

will help to give the full value.

The timing of dotted notes at a fast tempo can similarly tend to be slack. Making the dot almost a double dot tightens the rhythm and helps avoid a tendency to turn the rhythm into a lazy triplet with ♩♪ becoming almost ♩♪ Purcell's *Evening Hymn* can quickly lose its grip with the dotted rhythms soon developing into virtual triplets.

The rule is to always make a dot as long as you dare.

RHYTHM

Rhythm, the life pulse at the heart of all music, is very much part of what has just been said about note values. Everything that moves within a cycle of regularly recurring impulses is an aspect of rhythm, be it the *'tick* tock' of a clock, the *'left*, right, *left*, right' of marching, the seasons of the year, or the distinctive sound of an ambulance siren.

In more personal terms, without the security of a consistent and rhythmic beating of our heart and pulse, our stay in this world is likely to be a short one.

Yet, by some strange quirk, contrary to what would seem to be an instinctive part of our make-up, rhythm is a weak link in many a musician. While few of us would fail to be moved, often to considerable excitement, by a performance highly charged in rhythmic content (Beecham's recordings of Mozart for example), many of us seem totally unaware of our own personal shortcomings in this matter.

An equally tiresome part of human nature is the ability to see the shortcomings of others, but not our own.

Some of the guidelines towards ensuring rhythmic stability include such factors as

1 A compelling urge to 'feel' the pendulum swing from the strong beats to the weak beats, and *vice versa*. This is another aspect of what was mentioned on page 17

1	2	3	4
ONE	two	THREE	four

This applies with equal force whether the pulse be quick and where the rhythm should have an automatic vitality, or slow, when a broad lilt is called for.

2 Always work with as few main beats as possible. Three in a bar is usually more rhythmic when there is the instinctive 'feeling' of a broad swing on the first beat (ONE, two, three). Similarly four crotchets in a bar will frequently gain by becoming two minims. The hymn *Come, let us join our cheerful songs* is a good example. Whereas

can so easily sound fussy and lumpy

is more rhythmic, in that it emphasises the important words and syllables.

3 Words can be equally helpful in terms of ensuring rhythm—'Yet, day by day'. The more lightly 'by' is sung, the more obviously will the rhythm be felt on the two important words—'*day* by *day*'

4 It may seem strange to suggest that *the last beat of the bar is perhaps the most important beat of all*. Because it leads on to the first beat it is far too frequently shortened. The moral here is to give all 'up beats' *full* value.

From these obsrevations it can be seen that the style and personality of a performance will, to a large extent, be conditioned by such factors. Nor is it merely a matter of correct notes, full stop, as some would seem to think. Accuracy is only the start, leading on ideally to interpretation.

RESTS

Stanford is reputed to have said that rests are some of the
best moments in music. Be this as it may, failure to give
rests—and for that matter, long notes—their *full* value is
probably more prevalent than any other single rhythmic
shortcoming. Rests, as with long notes, may have been
counted but whether they are counted rhythmically and in
strict time is another matter. It is the speeding up of the
counting which results in the discrepancy.

Rests, as moments of silence, need to be 'felt' almost to
the extent of being stressed or emphasised as, for example,
in Parry's *I was glad*

$$\frac{4}{4} \left| \text{ vivat } \quad \text{REST } \quad \text{vivat } \quad \text{REST} \right|$$

*Finally, we must never confuse speed with vitality, or use it
as a substitute for rhythm. The two are by no means the
same.*

CHORDING AND BLEND

Both are linked in function and are virtually two ways of
looking at the same thing. As such, we shall discuss them
together with the one dependent on the other for the best
artistic result.

The accuracy of each constituent will be increased if *each*
voice (soprano, alto, tenor and bass in a normal four part
chord) listens to the other three parts. Singers are notoriously bad at hugging their own line and virtually closing
their ears to all else. They are so concerned with getting
their own lines correct that they fail to realise the help they
can gain, and to their advantage, from the other parts
around them.

As mentioned a few pages earlier, the third of the chord
must be emphasised. Whoever sings it gives the chord its

major or minor personality. Therefore thirds need to be slightly emphasised and coloured. This will help make the tuning accurate, especially the bright character of the major interval.

In the finer detail of really good choral singing, a chord of B flat will, because of spacing and the high tenor D have a much brighter quality than a more closely spaced chord of E.

In terms of real blend and the difficulties which can easily be encountered, the familar chant by Woodward is a classic example. Here, the relatively low soprano A is often swamped by the full onslaught of the tenors and basses in unison on a high D. To sing this chord with any sense of real balance calls for control and discipline as the men find the top D irresistible!

SATB in unison presents further difficulties, some of which are either glossed over or their potential not realised. To write off unison singing as easy is to beg the question. A glance at the comparative range of all four voices will show how difficult, even impossible, it is to arrive at a satisfactory compromise in which each part sings in a comfortable area of the voice. Add to this the distinct timbre of each of the four voices and there is a sizeable problem far greater than most choirmasters ever anticipate or concede.

Unison singing may rule out problems of chording but it creates other difficulties, not least in the blending together of four types of sound each with its distinctive and characteristic quality.

Never underestimate the problems of unison singing, not least in arriving at satisfactory tuning.

The number of voices in a choir is another factor which must always be taken into account. Many choirs are, for a variety of reasons, unbalanced. Nowadays a choirmaster thinks himself lucky to take what singers he can get and, as a result, seldom looks a gift horse in the mouth. Visually and psychologically, full choir stalls are a more attractive proposition than half empty ones.

A preponderance of tenors is especially dangerous, as tenors are frequently the chief culprits in singing flat. This may sometimes be because those who sing tenor are not really tenors at all. Equally, one flat tenor singing forcibly, and probably with a cutting edge, will quickly ruin any semblance of balance and chording.

Similarly, too soft a line will upset the balance in the opposite direction. It all reverts back to listening, and acting accordingly.

TONE AND DICTION

Here, the one is dependent on, and emerges out of, the other. Ninety per cent of good tone hinges on correct vowel sounds. Choir trainers do not always seem to realise this, or act on it. The remedy is simple if each unpleasant vowel sound is isolated, examined and corrected. Some examples will illustrate this:

1 '*How* – ly, *how* – ly, *how* – ly' will soon become '*Ho* – ly, *ho* – ly, *ho* – ly', when the lips are rounded and

the syllable 'ly' softened. Looking at a mirror and saying both versions will soon illustrate the correct way to proceed.

2 Diphthongs, or double vowels. As an example, break down the word 'praise'. By saying it slowly as *'pray – eese'* it is obvious that the first syllable is long and the second short. Then sing the word on a group of notes:

'Prayer' is another similar word in common church usage, and one frequently sung with incorrect vowel sounds. In this instance the first vowel sound must not change before the end of the word. 'Pop' singers are notorious at changing the vowel sound in the middle of a word:

'may – eeke' for 'make' and
'tay – eeke   for 'take'

In the same vein is 'lerve' instead of 'love', while 'therr'—with a straight mouth—does duty for 'the'. 'Iron' is a difficult word with a difference of opinion as to whether it is 'eyern' or 'eye – on'.

Consonants add the energy to the words. Lazy diction is common among singers, many of whom fail to realise the need for a neat and crisp approach to consonants. By the reverse token, it is wrong, and inartistic, to hear 'exploded' consonants, especially final ones, in soft singing. The word 'heart' is an example. If this is sung softly for four beats, the final 't'—which should sound on the fifth beat—needs to be quick and soft. It must never sound as 'har – *TER*'.

The word 'Ghost' can cause problems. Too often the 's' is so loud and long that the 't' is hardly heard. Ideally, both 's' and 't' should be quick and crisp, with equal stress on each and both sounded at the last possible moment.

'The' can be a lazy sound, but soon vitalised when the tongue shoots quickly between slightly parted teeth. This word, which often comes on a half-beat or up-beat, will be sluggish and unrhythmic unless it is pronounced in a slick way.

'Great' and 'glad' are examples of words commencing with double consonants. By saying 'ger–rate' and 'ger–lad' both consonants receive the equal prominence which is their due. Finally, 'Jesus', which needs to be pronounced as 'Chee – suss', or with the 'J' lengthened.

These are a few random examples but they illustrate important points of technique. Other words can be dealt with in a similar way as and when they arise.

Awareness for consonants and vowels produces good diction which, in its turn, helps rhythm.

The final sung phrase of Parry's *I was glad* is as good an example as any. With a combination of correct tuning, neat articulation, accents and precise dotted notes, you have the best of all possible worlds—and with an artistic end product into the bargain.

English is by no means the best language for singing. It has little of the guttural which underlines so much of German, or the 'musical' and lyrical emphasis of Italian.

Singers have to work hard to make something of the English language, the more so in soft singing when diction can become even more sluggish. It must also be borne in mind that in words of two syllables the first is usually stronger than the second, for example, '*Fa* – ther', '*glo* – ry', '*ev* – er', whereas in French the reverse obtains.

In most words of three syllables, it is the middle one which is emphasised: 'be – *gin* – ning' and 'temp – *ta* – tion'.

Phrasing is a further example of the combination of two factors—musical lines and words. The architectural outline, or shape, of musical phrases can be thought of in various ways. Best of all is probably a range of hills. If you take the second half of Sydney Nicholson's hymn tune *St Nicolas* there is a parallel with the line of the Malvern Hills going from south to north:

In looking at hills or mountains, the eye moves towards the peaks. So in music the energy, impulse and crescendo moves towards the high notes of the phrase and then down the other side.

A true phrase is an onward progression of notes in a parabola, never a mere collection of uneventful sounds lacking a sense of destination. The longer note values within a phrase are subject to a slight crescendo, either of tone or intensity:

The dependence of words on music, and *vice versa*, cannot be over emphasised. In the first phrase of Peter Aston's anthem *The True Glory* the word stresses take precedence over normal musical considerations:

(see also page 119)

The golden rule should be 'As you speak, so you sing'. Most of us, when talking in a natural voice, phrase without thinking. Surely the same ought always to be said of singing?

Our preoccupation with notes frequently precludes this, and does so to the detriment of the music. A result of the over-anxiety this creates is seen in an inability to produce a sustained cantabile. By the reverse token, a phrase is invariably thought of and interpreted as an unremitting legato. The presence of a slur over a group of notes would seem to emphasise this, but on many occasions detached notes are an essential part of a phrase, repeated notes being a case in point:

Sing his praise _____ with-out de-lays.

(Vaughan Williams: *Five Mystical Songs*)

Most of the quick quaver and semi-quaver runs in Bach and Handel come into the same category and are stylistically wrong if sung legato. Singers on the continent are more adept at this than their English counterparts.

A danger with repeated and detached notes is the urge to hurry them.

If the rhythm, and therefore the control, is assured, the performance, in terms of sparkle and excitement, is the greater.

Dynamics determine the colour, the *aural* counterpart to the beauty of *visual* colour all around us.

The complete range of tone between *ppp* and *fff* is seldom fully explored or realised, with choirs frequently resorting to a dull consistency ranging around *mf*.

It is so easy to sing fff and so hard to sing ppp.

The latter can invariably be the more exciting of the two, provided it is understood that soft singing needs just as much, or even more, energy in reserve as compared with loud singing.

Singers often misjudge the length of a crescendo when it is marked as applying to a long phrase. The extent of the crescendo must be carefully judged and then made to work out correctly, otherwise a choir can soon find it has reached its loudest well in advance of what is printed in the music.

While a crescendo may be a longish build up, the diminuendo down the other side is often comparatively quick.

Most singers find it much harder to diminuendo than to crescendo. In this respect, the amount of bow needed by a string player is a useful parallel in working this out.

The special effect of a *sfz* (sforzando) or an accent > can be produced either by a tonal 'stab' or through the words in question:

thun – der–eth

The control of a long soft note at the end of a phrase calls for care. Individual singers running short of breath should be encouraged to sneak a snatch breath as and when they need it. Through individual staggering of breath in this way the overall effect on the listener is that of one long sustained phrase, faked though it may perhaps be.

TEMPO

As compared with the other sections of this chapter, all of which deal with what ought to be indisputable fact, tempo is subject to an individual and personal interpretation. What follows should therefore be related to Chapter 2.

It is probably true to say that an incorrect choice of tempo can, for a variety of reasons, mar a performance more obviously than any other single factor.

How often, whether as performer or listener, our first reaction is 'Very nice, but if only it hadn't been quite so fast—or slow'.

We feel comfortable and secure, and therefore give a
more convincing performance, when we instinctively know
we have settled on the correct speed. This is dependent on a
number of factors:

1 The traditional Italian terms are open to a wide variety
of interpretation. Where slowness is concerned, Adagio,
Grave and Largo are frequently treated as all but
synonymous, yet each should surely have an individual
implication:

  Adagio = leisurely
  Grave = serious
  Largo = broad, or spread out

Vivace does not necessarily mean as fast as you can go,
this despite the widely held belief that vitality is equated
with break-neck speed. The Vivace marking in much
eighteenth-century German and Italian music, such as
the last movements of Haydn and Mozart symphonies
and sonatas, implies a sparkling and frequently detached
style with *rhythmic* vitality, rather than a mere excess of
speed as the guideline. Mere speed, even if allied to a
phenomenal technique which is meant to dazzle, soon
palls on the ear. When allied to a less than dazzling
technique, the chinks in the armour rapidly appear for all
to see.

What ultimately matters—and impresses—is rhythm,
not speed. That is why Sir Thomas Beecham was such a
profound conductor as revealed in his recordings.
Rhythm is the life blood of all musical endeavour.

2 Metronome markings are often, for some inexplicable
reason, notoriously unreliable as to what the composer
presumably intended. The reverse can also hold true, as
in the *Nunc Dimittis* of Stanford in A which is marked
Adagio. Whereas in itself ♩ = 52 is a reasonable enough
tempo, Adagio implies a much slower sense of movement.

3 To a certain extent, a building determines tempo. Even a

highly rhythmic Vivace with impeccable clarity of diction, can sound less than effective in resonant buildings such as St Paul's Cathedral, York Minster or Liverpool Cathedral. In such circumstances, excessively fast tempi will result in a gasping, and probably untidy, insecurity. Broader and slower tempi will be highly impressive, the more so when aligned to a generously sustained cantabile as and when this is needed.

4 The size and agility of the choir are further determining factors. *Messiah* and the *Mass in B minor* as sung by a small choir are generally a much more exciting proposition than the full blooded 300 strong chorus we may have once revelled in.

In terms of textual clarity and volume of sound, the smaller group is much nearer the resources known to the composer and probably what was in his mind when writing the music. By the reverse token, and for similar reasons, a small choir would under normal circumstances be unthinkable for Walton's *Belshazzar's Feast* or *The Dream of Gerontius*.

5 The distance between choir and organ is another factor which cannot be glossed over. Performance in a smallish chancel is a much easier proposition than the difficulties which can arise from a west end organ with the choir in the chancel.

6 A choir must learn to adjust in line with its size, the building, and the style of the music being sung. It cannot be reiterated too often how church choirs so easily fall into one style, one type of sound, and often one slavishly adopted tempo for virtually everything they sing. In this context, it is akin to, and maybe influenced by, the unimaginative diapason-based registration which is the *ad nauseam* norm of many an organist.

7 If the tempo is too slow, it is impossible to sing without creating breathing problems which, in their turn, make it

so difficult, if not impossible, to relay the shape of a phrase.

8 In respect of hymns, some are played at such a speed, and with so little breathing space between verses, that all concerned—certainly me as a member of a congregation most Sundays—derive little edification from the exercise. The same applies in reverse to laboriously slow hymns, the more so when the parson, in an effort to liven up the service, sings loudly.

I am not sure which is the worse or lesser evil. Both leave one breathless, if for different reasons. One thing is certain—*every hymn has its own speed and its own character*. Some organists subscribe to a 25 mph speed limit, be it Christmas Day or mid-Lent, while some clergy mistakenly believe that a breathless pursuit of hymnody, willy nilly, will help 'jolly up' a service. For most of us it has the reverse effect for we surely go to church for a different type of stimulation which, alas, is not always forthcoming.

9 Two specific examples concerning tempi, probably as much as anything, are

1 The tendency to hurry a succession of quick notes, such as is found in much Haydn, Mozart and Handel, and on one vowel sound. A better control can usually be achieved if the notes are slightly detached from each other (see page 26).

2 Phrases such as

Sing his praise_____

(Vaughan Williams: *Five Mystical Songs*)

where the first two notes must be detached yet rhythmically secure. Tudor church music abounds in variants of this, especially with the interval of the rising fourth, as in *Rejoice in the Lord alway* (see page 66).

What then is the correct tempo? As a generally reliable guide, one bar of quick notes will usually indicate this as, for example, bars 8 and 9 of the *Magnificat* of Walmisley in D minor.

BALANCE WITH THE ORGAN

This is experienced as something of a two-way traffic. A choir which sings too loudly cannot hear the organ and usually, because of the energy being put into the singing, tends to sharpen in pitch. In much the same way, the organist who plays too loudly, as can so often happen, forces the choir to keep up in volume of equal terms.

The other side of this particular coin is the organist who does not provide enough support. An anaemic and colourlessly reluctant registration is just as much a deterrent to good singing as is an overpoweringly loud accompaniment. The effects of both are felt just as much by the congregation as by the choir.

The answer to these particular problems lies much more with the organist as an individual than with the choir as a group of people. While it is obvious that bright registration is a must for rhythmic and lively music, a richer choice of sounds should prevail where more sustained singing is concerned.

The organist frequently fails to realise that what seems correct at the console is often less agreeable in the body of the church. He also often fails to realise that in many instances the swell is buried at the back of the organ with much of its power lost to the congregation.

The moral is for the organist to sometimes forsake his console and hear for himself the effect in the body of the church where the majority of those on the receiving end are sitting. He will then soon learn, as I have done, that what seems right at the console, is hopelessly out of gear elsewhere.

4

The influence of the organist as an accompanist

Accompanying is a partnership. The true accompanist is a servant helping through expertise and musicianship to produce a better and more complete performance. The chances are that in the process this will inspire, an ideal that applies just as much to the village organist playing hymns as to Gerald Moore accompanying Fischer-Dieskau in a Schubert song-cycle.

The influence of the accompanist is immense, frequently under-estimated but often entered into lightly. The good accompanist aids but never dominates; the worst type of accompanist mars a performance. It's as realistic as that.

In terms of the church service where resources may seldom be those of the Gerald Moore calibre, awareness of values are no less called for. At some time or another all of us have suffered from an organist who either pulls us along, far too loudly and with a breathless pursuit, or he who discreetly follows half a beat or more behind. Neither is accompanying.

The potential for good or bad is enormous, the more so when we consider how the organ can dominate through sheer volume of sound, even to the extent of a take-over bid, be it intentionally or otherwise.

HYMNS (and to a considerable extent, psalms)

The average church organist is likely during his life to play more hymns than anything else, for hymns are the staple and often inescapable diet of music in worship. Whether, in the process, the organist inspires those on the receiving end, leaves no positive impression, or drives choir and congregation to desperation, is another matter.

This influence commences with the play-over which is designed to put us in the picture by reminding us of the tune and its tempo. It should also aim to project the character and mood of the hymn which, in the best circumstances, will be done in a subtle and convincing way. How often, in reality, it is routine and unimaginative. This also has its influence as will the countless instances where the speed of the introduction bears little rhythmic relationship to what follows or where great hymns of praise are played over as lethargic bedtime lullabies.

The play-over of a hymn must be construed as much a setter of pace and mood as is the introduction to a song.

Following on from this are such complementary matters as registration mirroring the text—and that does not suggest a slavish adherence to some of the excesses to be found in certain hymn books, such as 'in life' (loud), 'in death' (very soft—and probably much slower!). It does mean thinking about the text—and in advance—and deciding how best to relay the overall mood of a hymn, verse by verse, where the textual climaxes come and where there are moments for reflection. 'The head that once was crowned with thorns' is a particularly good illustration of this.

In terms of pace and rhythm, the organist, no less than the choir, needs to consider what is mentioned on page

44, namely, when a firm four-in-a-bar is needed or when, as in 'Blest are the pure in heart', two-in-a-bar produces a more realistic flow.

Having decided on this and having put it into motion in the play-over, he will quickly influence for good his choir and congregation. But—for better or sometimes worse—it all stems from the organist, as the accompanist, subtly suggesting by example and wanting in the process to create an impressionable reaction.

The sensible accompanist, be it in conducting opera or playing for a folk song or simple hymn, will himself go through the motions of singing. By doing this, relatively few of the otherwise potential problems are likely to arise over such matters as punctuation while that deplorable disease of giving virtually no breathing space between verses will be eliminated. The mechanics of breathing, in terms of a singer, takes time. The organist, whose instrument breathes electrically, does not always realise this.

The discerning accompanist will lead a reluctant congregation without making it all that obvious. Pulling out more and more stops and bullying a choir and congregation through sheer force of noise will have little effect, except to discourage and ultimately make all concerned give up in despair. Detaching the right hand and playing rhythmically will quickly help to produce the desired effect—and —through legitimate artistic means.

Other subtleties follow, such as playing 'over the top'. In most music the accompanist frequently weaves a line independent to that of the melody with its contours deriving from the basic harmonic structure, but with the subtle addition of passing notes and sometimes suspensions.

Because a hymn tune is written out in a prescribed way, it does not always occur to an organist to do anything but slavishly mirror what the voices sing. Take *Franconia* as a random example, where

might become

This is but one of a number of ways in which this and many other tunes can be treated.

Similarly, where the singing is fully SATB, or where everyone is singing in unison, the accompaniment for certain verses need not always be in four parts:

The main point at issue here is not to merely play the voice parts at written pitch from start to finish in every hymn and psalm. Otherwise the accompaniment is so unadventurous, unvarying and, in the final count, inartistic. Some variety at least, even if it is confined to the final verse of a hymn, adds to the overall interest of the listener.

From this, it is but an extension to think in terms of a free accompaniment to a unison verse, final or elsewhere. But—to do this 'off the cuff' is an ability given to relatively few. The guideline here, as I have frequently said elsewhere, is not to tamper around with the original unless you can legitimately and artistically better what is already there.

There are a number of collections of free accompaniments available. Even if some are of varying artistic merit, there is no excuse for trying your luck on the spur of an unprepared moment and on unsuspecting victims. Great can be your fall.

ANTHEMS AND SERVICE SETTINGS

In many instances the accompaniment here is independent of the voice parts. From this, certain factors emerge which throw a measure of responsibility on to the organist. It is not merely setting the correct tempo and using the right stops for an introduction, but helping from the outset to transmit the mood and character of the music through such means as colour, style and rhythm, three important characteristics which help to single out the organ part as distinct from what the voices are doing. In this way an ideal partnership emerges.

It may be that the accompaniment will have its own individual pattern, often in note values faster than the voices. Bach's *Jesu, joy of man's desiring* and the soprano section 'Love one another' from S. S. Wesley's *Blessed be the God and Father* are two such examples. The latter is a hybrid one, with the continuous succession of quavers demanding neat articulation, especially when they come in the centre of the chordal structure.

In other instances the accompaniment will be more sustained than the voice parts, as in the ensuing recitative in the Wesley anthem. More often than not it is a combination of both, as in Britten's exhilarating *Jubilate* where the organ part, through its highly charged individuality, complements the voice parts and *vice versa*. In music such as this the accompaniment is as important and integral a feature of the whole, as are the voices. The two independently combine to produce a total experience.

As with the various devices used to provide orchestral colour, so the organist has to use distinctive stops or groups of stops to produce the necessary colour, while at the same time achieving a correct tonal balance with the choir. In the main, mutations will be needed for rhythmic and sparkling accompaniments, with diapasons and reeds being generally used for more sustained passages.

It will not do merely to resort to pistons, these being only part of the picture, however necessary, in terms of a large instrument. Imaginative accompaniment needs equal imagination and forethought in the use of stops, with the size and consequent tonal ambience of the choir another factor which, in terms of balance, must be taken fully into account.

Another aspect arising from this is how to deal with orchestral accompaniments written out on two staves. Take, as an example, Schubert's *The Lord is my shepherd* or *How lovely is thy dwelling place* from Brahms' Requiem. In both instances it would be impossible—and undesirable—to play note for note what is there. Even if it could be managed, the result would be far from satisfactory, for what works in terms of the wide spread of the piano keyboard and helped by the sustaining pedal, is entirely out of place when transferred to the organ. It can even sound ludicrous.

Sir William Harris, who was little short of a genius at making this type of piano accompaniment sound highly convincing when transferred to the organ, always said 'It's not what you play that matters, but what you leave out'. He would go on to show that the left hand, by playing sustained triads at the appropriate moments, fulfils the same unifying function as that of the woodwind and horns in a romantic score.

The accompanist, no less than the choirmaster and the singers, is an integral part of making church music work. A dull, routine approach will quickly act as a deterrent to a choir and congregation as will an imaginative and stylish approach inspire all concerned. This is what surely matters.

Nor has the accompanist only himself to consider. Far

from it, for in certain situations there will be a conductor whose beat must be law. The organist who watches the conductor for the first few beats and then goes his own way lamely following (he will seldom get in front) and with his eyes glued to the music, is obviously a hindrance to all concerned.

The conscientious accompanist knows his notes so well that his eyes will be on the conductor at every awkward corner while anticipating each and every time change.

As the accompanist has the first word, and probably the last one as well, he can make a dull organ sound alive and interesting; he can also transmit vitality and a feeling that he instinctively wants to make an influence for good. The good accompanist will not write off hymns and psalms as necessary evils but will view them as more important than a virtuoso performance of the final voluntary. And—his voluntary before the service can similarly act as something having considerable significance and influence on the service.

5

The influence of the conductor

Any music making on a group basis usually demands some measure of overall direction. This, in the first instance, is to control and co-ordinate the forces. Imagine the free for all of a Brahms' symphony, an Elgar oratorio or a Wagner opera without a conductor.

In the concert hall, and in terms of a professional orchestra where highly skilled performers are involved, the function of the conductor is to interpret, not to teach notes. What he sets out to communicate in rehearsal is brought to fruition in performance where, through a combination of gesture and, not least, personality, he relays to the players his personal and individual interpretation of the score.

The fact that no two people approach a work in identical terms is surely more than half the fun of the game for performers and listeners alike. Denied this the critic would soon be out of business, for there would be nothing for him to criticise; nor would the listener be able to make the comparisons between one performance and another, this latter an integral part of any artistic endeavour.

In terms of the average church choir, different criteria

are likely to apply, the points of departure being the learning of notes, the available resources and, with this, the ability of the singers. These are considerations which should play no small part in determining the choice of repertoire.

Even so, the fundamental common denominator, that of performance at the highest possible level of endeavour, should in every respect be identical, be it the Vienna Boys' Choir or a village group of all ages, shapes and sizes singing the simplest of music as part of the Sunday worship in their church.

Being amateur is no reason for accepting a lower standard of values, merely a convenient excuse for sins of omission and not bothering to take trouble.

In terms of practicalities, correctness of notes both in pitch and length, and clarity of diction, are disciplines which must be common points of departure, and which any self-respecting choirmaster will have to emphasise again and again, persevering until he gets the required standard of result. He must be prepared to work at these skills to a far greater extent than the conductor of a highly experienced professional orchestra or choir.

Finer points, such as chording, balance, dynamic range, and rhythmic awareness, are ingredients which not only underline the performance of the better choirs, but are essentials to any completely satisfying performance.

The choir trainer who has his wits about him and who seeks integrity will, through his interpretative powers, carry these matters a stage further, indicating by gesture the speeds, time changes, pauses and dynamics he wants—and which he feels to be essential to a full understanding of the composer's intentions. Through his sense of musicianship, these ingredients produce what we believe to be performance in its fullest sense. This applies to a simple hymn as much as to an ornate anthem.

The one contingency which cannot be legislated for is the degree of inner perception which marks out certain conductors and certain choir trainers. There are, as St Paul so aptly reminded us, diversities of gifts. If there were not, there would be little incentive in art and no yardstick by which to measure the inexplicable satisfaction we derive from genius. The true artist and, for that matter, the true performer will each in his or her turn seek to be inspired by the genius of a Janet Baker, a von Karajan, a Guilini and a Barenboim. Not least in all this is the stimulus we lesser mortals derive from those endowed with great artistic gifts.

Beating time, as we so oddly term it, is in its own right a necessary function to keep a choir together—but—it is not an end in itself as some conductors would seem to have us believe. Nor should it be viewed as a matter of course that *all* church music, accompanied or not, should automatically be conducted. Many a choir will gain a lot from having to listen to each other and make convincing music without the aid of a conductor.

Having stressed these important fundamentals, a number of points now need to be considered:

1 *The mechanics of getting a choir started* and indicating this in such a way as to produce the confidence necessary from the outset. The preliminary, extra beat which prefaces the actual start of the music has two important functions, it visibly alerts the singers and should be an automatic reaction for the taking of breath. It is as necessary for the singer as for the wind player; it also allows the string player time to get his bow poised over the string. It follows that the best conductors breath with their singers. Equally fundamental, this preliminary beat *must be at exactly the speed at which the music is to move*. Some conductors seem oblivious to the need for clearly indicating the start. Whereas they will probably curse their singers for an untidy or hesitant start, the chances are that the fault is the conductor's, and his alone.

2 *Much the same applies to the ending*. Unless this is

equally clearly indicated, and prepared for, the singers have little idea of what is happening or when the end will come. This is the more so when the final note is on a pause. If the final word ends with a consonant, the need for an unmistakably clear cut-off is even more necessary.

3 Conductors frequently fail to appreciate that *clarity of gesture* is not only conducive to more confident singing but is a necessity where a group of people are corporately concerned in a common pursuit. The fact that many a famous orchestral conductor can be faulted on this point of technique is neither here nor there. Sir John Barbirolli could be notorious in this respect. He once said to me 'If the beat isn't clear they have to listen to each other much more, and that's good for them'. True—but he was dealing with highly experienced professional musicians.

4 *The conductor who is also an organist* may sometimes forget that when he puts his hands down on the keys there is an instantaneous mechanical reaction denied to singers whose vocal mechanism is considerably slower to react.

5 From this, it is but a small step onwards to the necessity for *the conductor to phrase with his singers*, feeling the shape of a phrase through his gesture. In this way, important words and notes will be given their due emphasis, with less significant words treated more lightly:

The left hand can help by indicating important words and syllables with, through an increase of gesture, the necessary melodic shape on and through to the last note, which is the melodic and rhythmic culmination of the phrase.

The same applies just as much to breathing, as was mentioned just now. Breathing and punctuation are an integral part of phrasing, and *vice versa*. Some give and take is necessary where the physical process of breathing is concerned. This must be allowed for at those points in the music where strict time will cause a gasp or an untidy join:

Our glor-ious God. To praise His name

* should be slightly longer than a crotchet beat. A rubato effect will help any problems here over the necessity of taking breath.

6 *Style can often be indicated to the singers through the hands.* A flowing cantabile, such as in the hymn 'The King of love my shepherd is', calls for a correspondingly legato and flowing beat, while a more detached marcato style, as in 'Come, ye faithful, raise the anthem' will be relayed to advantage through a more determined and rhythmically urgent use of the hands.

7 In church it is generally best to give *a small beat*. Quite apart from there being no justification or need for the kind of gesture needed for a 200 strong choral society singing the *Hallelujah Chorus*, a large beat is distracting to the congregation. This is the more so if the conductor is in full view in a chancel two or three steps above the level of the congregation. Every movement is far more visible than he probably realises.

The importance of the first beat in each bar should be slightly emphasised and, to a lesser extent, the third beat in quadruple time. This will help the rhythm, while undue emphasis on the less important beats merely encourages the singers to plod on solidly. *Such is the power of the conductor.*

8 In music which is moving along with an assured security, it is sometimes useful merely to *beat the rhythm*:

or to beat the important words and syllables:

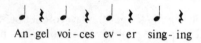

An-gel voi-ces ev-er sing-ing

The fewer the beats, the more convincingly will the music flow. He who makes every beat identical and probably heavy, jerky and cumbersome into the bargain, cannot complain if his singers react similarly. They are also the more likely to watch an economy of gesture which demands far more concentration than a beat which is visible throughout the length and breadth of the church.

SOME FINER POINTS:

Given that the conductor relays what he wants through both clarity and a minimum of gesture, other factors can enhance a performance even further:

1 The *independent* use of the left hand to indicate crescendos, diminuendos and entries, to reinforce the right hand for starts, stops, changes of tempo and, not least, for turning pages.
   Always remember that the prime task of the right hand is

to indicate the pulse. The left hand has its own particular
tasks; it should never merely mirror the right.
The less the left hand is used, the more effective it will
be.

2 It is reasonably safe to assume that in all probability most
of the singers will be watching the conductor far more
than he realises. The wise conductor will want to use his
face as well as his hands. He may be feeling the mood of
joyful music but he will not relay it by scowling.

3 All these matters presuppose one important consideration, that of knowing the music and consequently being
able to conduct without your head continuously buried
in the score. The problem with singers and conductors is
that the score holds a fatal fascination, even a magnet-
ism, which compels us to look at it far more than is
necessary. Many of the best performances are those
from memory when the communication between conductor and performers is complete and when the attention of all concerned is focussed on making music without the continual distraction of looking down at a printed
page.
Conducting from memory also helps to increase the
confidence of the singers (and the conductor) and with it
comes an instinctively infectious group feeling that all
concerned are going to give the more easily of their best.
To suggest this is surely not asking all that much, the
more so considering that the average piece of church
music bears no comparison with the length and complex-
ity of a symphony, many of which frequently receive
their best performances when conducted from memory.

4 Certain practicalities, arising from different situations,
may need to be taken into account. The size of the choir,
where it is situated in relation to the organ, whether the
choir can hear the organ, and *vice versa*, are factors
which may determine the advisability of having a conductor, especially for music which may present special

rhythmic or tonal demands. It is of some relevance to reflect that in Liverpool Cathedral the two sides of the choir are spaced so far apart that they cannot possible keep together without a conductor.

WHERE SHOULD THE CONDUCTOR STAND?

The middle of the chancel is seldom desirable or necessary. It is usually best to stand on the side opposite the organ console and at the west end of the choir stalls. The back view of the conductor is usually less off-putting than seeing his face; it also means that if the choir slightly turn towards the conductor, the singing will be directed towards the body of the church.

In this position it may be necessary to use both hands to 'embrace' both sides of the choir. Even so, a minimum of gesture should always be the order of the day.

Finally, one or two general matters:

1 The art of conducting, however small or great the resources may be, is only learned by the experience of actually doing it. Knowing what is wrong, being able to right this, knowing what you want in terms of perform-ance, and persevering until you get it, are all factors in the process.

2 A church service is not a concert. Any affectation, how-ever much personal satisfaction may derive from aping André Previn or Adrian Boult, is an inescapable distrac-tion to those in full view on the receiving end, unless they elect to bury their heads in their hands.

3 As with the playing of the organist, it is the relaying of personality which in the end will be the determining factor. Some choirmasters merely have to look at their choir to claim their whole-hearted attention while others wave and flap their arms to little or no account.

The real conductor is able to inspire his forces as an

automatic part of his innate musicianship. In the process, he will not have to rely on gimmicks or a power complex.

4 There are many occasions on which a conductor is by no means necessary or desirable and when a choir will sing just as well by having to look across at each other—and listen to each other—this latter something often glossed over or underestimated in its importance.

6

How to choose the music

It is not so much a matter of what we would like to do—and this includes those we might like to impress in the process—as a number of fundamental issues which, if we are wise, must determine everything.

First come the resources. These, as mentioned elsewhere in this book, must be the point of departure. This means the extent of the local talent available week by week, together with their capabilities. A choir with an average age of sixty plus and weaned on Stainer and Barnby is a factor which, give or take a little, is as much to be contended with as the choir so brain-washed that anything remotely post-Stanford is anathema. Try selling Rutter, Mathias, even Vaughan Williams, to a choir rooted in such a tradition and you will swiftly meet your musical Waterloo.

Many choir members subscribe to the belief that simple music is *infra dig*. In other words, they must of necessity bite off more than they can comfortably chew and irrespective of the consequences of what may be inflicted on the unsuspecting listener.

Probably the hardest single factor in all this is that of making a choir aware of its limitations. Given half a chance, choirmasters are equally guilty of encouraging their choirs to embark on music beyond their capabilities and which they themselves are sometimes unable to teach properly. When neither choirmaster nor choir are aware of their limitations, they are usually blind, and often deaf, to the realisation that what they foist on the congregation is the very reverse of an enrichment to worship.

Having said this, there is the other side of the coin, that of the need to challenge a choir and make it aware of what it could probably achieve within its capabilities, providing it rehearses adequately and is rehearsed correctly.

I have often quoted the ill-assorted collection of singers which comprised the Dartmoor village church choir and their bid to 'have a go' at an 8-part Palestrina anthem (in Latin) which the choirmistress chanced to hear when visiting King's College, Cambridge. This was as much part of my experience when I was organist of Exeter Cathedral as was that of my next door neighbour, the Bishop of Crediton, who on more than one occasion peered over my garden wall in the Close (we were both keen gardeners) to tell me of his experiences the previous night when confirming in rural Devon. 'They had learned *Blessed be the God and Father* specially because I was to be there. I do wish they hadn't!'

This phobia to impress for its own sake gets us nowhere, least of all the choir and the choirmaster. It merely creates false illusions of grandeur; sooner or later someone is bound to come along and prick this particular balloon.

The excuse put forward by some choirs that their existing repertoire is inhibiting and that they therefore opt for more weighty fare is a lame excuse. It may or may not be true. The six- or eight-part anthem would seem to be a status symbol exemplifying a misplaced sense of priorities. It is merely a perverted sense of values which dictates that a choir stubbornly cling to music which is of cathedral dimensions and which will probably only sound fully convincing when performed by a cathedral choir.

While I have every admiration for many of those who valiantly play organs or sing in choirs, especially those who play because no one else is available, I quickly part company with geriatrics who are long past coping with the task and refuse to accept the fact, either by their own volition, or, worse still, because the parson wishes to avoid a rumpus by suggesting that such a person retires from the scene. This dodging the issue merely serves to heap up coals of fire, to alienate and even to lose others from the choir who have standards and wish to see their gifts used towards a more positive and realistic end-product.

There is no justification whatever in putting off the evil day. All of us eventually pass our period of usefulness and even if we do not, or will not, come to terms with it, we must not be surprised if others grasp this particular nettle and put us out to grass. To placate someone who is past it gets no one anywhere. In a similar way, the long service choir member, once he or she has passed the limit, is hard to dislodge, for there is always the carrot of boasting a number of years in a choir.

While all of us are anxious and ready to applaud long service, merely to hold on in order to have the personal satisfaction of clocking up more years than is healthy should be neither condoned nor encouraged. *'To all men* (and women) *there comes a time and a place. . .'*

Moving on now to a more detailed assessment, it is indefensible to propose that because you wish to sing an anthem which includes two tenor parts, and you are light on the tenor line, a bass can 'have a shot' at one of the two tenor lines. Those who boast of an ability to sing alto, tenor, or bass as required usually produce a strange, even unhealthy, sound on at least one of the registers, if not on all of them. Is it all that surprising? The human voice, by its very nature, is not normally quite that versatile.

Nowadays there is plenty of interesting music available, much of it for limited, even depleted, resources.

Long playing records are in many respects an unreliable

guide to our choice of repertoire. They give the impression that it is all so easy, both vocally and instrumentally, a utopia which is soon dispelled when it comes to practicalities.

What is sung at any specific moment in any service must ultimately be dependent on its suitability to the occasion, to the church and its particular congregation. You just cannot twist a small repertoire and make believe it will do for any occasion. The chinks in this particular armour will soon reveal themselves to those on the receiving end even though the performers may themselves be oblivious.

If, as an example of this, you cannot find an anthem suitable to the Feast of St Gertrude of Battersea, it is wide of the mark to sing Stanford's *How beauteous are their feet* merely because this is a Saint's Day anthem. This sort of misrepresentation can easily happen but the connection between the one and the other must be rather less tenuous.

It is indefensible nowadays to suggest, as do some of the clergy, that an anthem with a Latin text is 'high church' and therefore must not be sung in a context where the persuasion is evangelical. Surely it is far more honest to use the text which the composer set instead of what may well be a watered down translation which, although it may fit the music, bears little or no connection with the original. The alternative English words in the Novello edition of Arcadelt's *Ave Maria* is a prime example of this.

If, as a choirmaster, you are at all uncertain over such matters, do seek the advice of those who can help. It can avoid your making a howler.

What you eventually decide on must fit into the needs of the church and the season. It must be the result of careful forward planning and thought, with the sum total of music involved over a period of time spaced out in a realistic and practical way so as to allow adequate rehearsal time. The menu must have variety. Penitence must be contrasted with praise, old with modern and quick with slow, all of which will contribute towards giving the choir a broadminded outlook and the experience of choral dexterity.

But—and this is a very big but—this can only fully materialise when everything is sung in its correct mood and style, not ironed out into a dull monotony of uniformity. It is so unimaginative to hear, as happens so frequently, an example of seventeenth-century florid polyphony sung with the same tone and in the same style as Stanford's *Beati quorum via*. This lack of discernment even applies to some cathedral choirs who should know better.

A little imagination, while at the same time taking into account certain practical factors, will help to produce an end-product with a conviction of performance which will ring true and fit into each occasion like a glove.

Length is something which must constantly be borne in mind. Edifying though it may be for a choir to enjoy themselves singing a communion motet which is far too long, the effect will be very different on the parson and congregation eagerly waiting to get on with a service which is only too obviously being delayed and prolonged.

The use of hymns as anthems presents a number of possibilities. The wealth of interesting supplements in use today provides much useful material in this respect, with a number of examples more readily choir pieces than congregational items. John Wilson's collection of *Sixteen Hymns of Today for Use as Anthems* (published by the RSCM) shows a novel approach while at the same time providing eminently practical examples which are by no means difficult to sing or play.

The Psalms—A New Translation for Worship (Collins Liturgical Publications) can also be used to advantage as choir pieces. As a new translation in contemporary language this Psalter is likely to be linked with the 1980 Alternative Services Book. It is *not* a substitute for the familiar Coverdale version, merely an alternative. It would therefore seem sensible to use some of the shorter psalms, or portions of psalms, as Introits, Graduals, and Communion motets, or in their own right in specially contrived services.

HOW DO YOU CHOOSE?

Your own library may contain much that is good and some that is less enviable. It may even be the other way round. In either instance there is likely to be a fair smattering of Victoriana. Most repertoires need periodic enlarging and widening. How do you set about it? The dearth of publishers' catalogues, the meagreness of what is being generally published today, and the lack of music shops in which to browse, combine to make it far from easy to find out exactly what is available. No sooner do you find something than the chances are it will go out of print.

One answer is to pick other people's brains and take every opportunity of finding out for yourself. Others are likely to do the same where you are concerned. Because of these intrinsic difficulties, a soft option is to find oneself ending up with the puny and worthless, however highly motivated your intentions might originally have been. The problem may be further increased through no two people necessarily agreeing on the relative value of one piece as compared with another.

A fairly reliable thermometer is that of the generally accepted guidelines. More church music than we often realise, especially that of the nineteenth century, is a turgid and uneventful succession of chords with movement devoid of what we understand to be vocal interest. Many examples in this category are little more than organ chords with words added—and probably conceived in that order. Whatever the words may be, little account may have been taken of the text unless it is made the excuse for a word painting extravaganza. Much of it will represent one style, and a not very good one at that. At its best much will be deadly dull, at its worst plain uninspired.

With so much on the debit side it calls for a sensitive and

well drilled choir to make much impact. It will be hard work
with few satisfactory returns at the end of this particular
road.

Obviously not all the music of this period comes into this
damning category. There are notable exceptions, of which
Goss's hauntingly beautiful *O Saviour of the world* and
King Solomon's Prayer—*O Lord my God*—by S. S.
Wesley, are but two random instances.

In fairness to the nineteenth-century scene we must
remember that Victorian church musicians knew virtually
no Tudor music. The position of privilege in which we find
ourselves today provides a very different set of conditions.
The wealth of rediscovered music of Tudor and other
periods which is so readily accessible to us today was almost
completely denied to church musicians in the nineteenth
century. Add to this the tremendous strides made during
the past eighty years in terms of composition, which means
repertoire and opportunities for hearing so much music
superbly performed, and you have a state of affairs far beyond the wildest dreams of those who lived in the nineteenth
century. Because these are realities so easily within our
grasp, do we sometimes take them for granted?

Nor must we confine these strictures and comparisons
solely to the nineteenth century which, on balance, does
tend to be maligned without reserve. By no means every
twentieth-century composer is immune from the charge of
writing dull music. Although to a certain extent some of the
less desirable elements in church music composition have
now been eradicated, some aspects do linger on and in
enough areas of activity to spell out a situation which is not
always encouraging.

Much of the problem in this and every generation lies in
the fact that in church music so much revolves around
association. We are constantly faced with a sentimental
regard for this and that which can effectively outweigh
artistic considerations. To hark back once more to the
Victorians, their choice of texts was frequently third rate.

As an example of both sides of this particular coin we have only to look at Stainer's *Crucifixion* where the words of the hymns obviously inspired the composer much more than the less than satisfactory narrative which in its turn produced music of a generally low calibre.

A further factor is that much of the English church music of the past 150 years has been, and continues to be, written not so much by *bona fide* composers as by the amateur who has always found an easy outlet, and a ready platform, in the Church. The urgency to rush into print was a carrot many nineteenth-century composers could not resist; it is a weakness which has bedevilled church music and retarded its growth and which is in marked contrast to the professionalism which generally underlines the composition of secular music.

Today, and this is much more to the point, one of our greatest assets is the encouraging number of composers who are in no way officially connected with the Church yet elect to write for it. Much of the resulting originality is evidence of an encouraging 'new look' seen in a lively regard for highly charged rhythms and a colourful harmonic scheme, both calculated to capture the interest and attention of discerning choirs. Nor are energy, vitality and overall interest confined to quick music; far from it as witness the music of Herbert Howells, much of which is slowish but packed full of these attributes.

This makes it the harder to generate enthusiasm which will create much sense out of four square Victoriana. The fact that choirs do persist in this is as much a reflection of the attitude of mind of the choir and its choirmaster as it is a reflection of the music itself.

There are no short cuts in the search for the right choice of music. Having found examples, there should of necessity be an element of experimentation, even if this ultimately means rejection. The widening of sights and finding the right repertoire should be a constant process.

The list of anthems which follows makes not attempt to

be exhaustive. There will be omissions and inclusions which some may find surprising. It nevertheless presents a broadly based and carefully thought out selection which should act as a useful overall guideline. Having chosen the music is one matter and relatively easy as compared with *how* you elect to interpret it. This end-product, the object of the exercise, must always be uppermost in our minds.

7

How to rehearse

(This section is intended to be read in conjunction with *Starting from scratch* on page 147).

Having all too frequently witnessed what were doubtless the well-intentioned efforts of many a choir trainer—even if they were all to no avail—I am left in no doubt that the root cause is a misplaced rehearsal procedure which, in most instances, is combined with a lack of know how, first in planning out a rehearsal, and then in making the best use of the available time.

Text book knowledge is one thing, being able to put it across in a productive way another matter.

While we all admire those who are prepared to give up an evening or two each week to attend a choir practice, those concerned do at least expect to see some return for their efforts. Merely to sing through next Sunday's music is of little value in itself. There must be systematic teaching and, with it, a feeling of wellbeing induced by the fact that some improvement in the standard of technical proficiency and performance has obtained as a result of each and every rehearsal.

A choir will naturally be thwarted if it feels it is getting nowhere. When this state of affairs prevails for weeks and

57

months on end, the sense of frustration will be acute as will be the absence of the obvious enjoyment which through achievement should be an added bonus for one's efforts.

The answer to all these matters rests solely with the choirmaster. The main faults would seem to lie in two directions, firstly the lack of a systematic rehearsal plan which has been worked out well in advance and not played by ear on the spur of the moment as the rehearsal proceeds. This must be linked with a teaching method which not only immediately corrects any mistakes but, more importantly, builds up an equally systematic increase of proficiency which in its turn creates confidence. This latter is surely at the heart of the matter.

Suggestions on general arrangements for a rehearsal were dealt with at some length in my book *Church Music at the Crossroads* (Marshall, Morgan and Scott, 1970). This is now out of print, but as I constantly meet and see in action those who tell me how useful they found the book yet seem to put few, if any, of the ideas into practice, I feel it might perhaps be helpful to reiterate some of the headings.

1 The need to plan a rehearsal with plenty of variety in mind. For example, joyful music, preferably as a starter, to be followed by something more reflective. Quick music might be alternated with slow music and loud with soft.

2 *Priorities must always come before personal preferences*. Therefore rehearse first things first; that means hymns which are the bread and butter.

3 To start a rehearsal with a good 'sing' produces a sense of doing something. The surest way to ensure a dull rehearsal is to begin with the *Nunc Dimittis*—softly and slowly.

4 Difficult or new music should be worked at in the first half of a rehearsal while the singers are fresh.

5 Only rehearse what is necessary.

6 As too much loud singing will tire a choir, and probably
   cause the pitch to sharpen, so will a surfeit of soft
   singing contribute towards flatness.

7 If attention flags it usually means you have spent too
   long on one thing and need to move on to something
   entirely different.

8 Avoid unnecessary talking. A choir has come primarily
   to sing. Therefore say what you have to briefly and
   explicitly.

9 A businesslike attitude must prevail. A rehearsal
   packed full of activity will pay dividends.

10 Finally, if a rehearsal is meant to last one hour, it should
   last no more. If you get to the end of the hour and find
   you have not been through everything, something has
   gone wrong with your timetable.

For those who wish to elaborate on these topics, they are
dealt with on pages 46 to 55 of my earlier book.

Before moving on to deal with specific examples there
are certain guidelines which must of necessity determine
any reliable point of basic departure, whatever the music
may be. These can be summarised as:

1 Correctness of notes and time must be the first priority.
   This means that from the outset any awkward notes,
   rhythms, intervals and accidentals must be pinpointed,
   isolated, and systematically corrected. This not only
   engenders security but helps towards greater confidence. Too often such matters are not grappled with and
   sorted out in the early stages of learning.

2 Diction. Choirs do not always realise how essential the
   clarity of articulation must be if what is being sung is to
   convey anything intelligible to the listener.
   Nor is it always understood that diction must be the
   clearer where a number of people are involved. This
   demands that *choral* diction be consciously exaggerated,

the more so as we English, as compared with Germans and Italians, are notoriously guilty of lazy speech.

3 Expression marks. The range of permutations between *pp* and *ff* is enormous and seldom fully exploited. The same can be said with regard to giving full colour to each and every $<$ $>$ bearing in mind the extent of long and short crescendos. A dull sameness, usually revolving around a drab *mf*, is too often the order of the day. This undoubtedly contributes towards the difficulties which many choirs encounter when trying to sing *pp*.

These then are some of the essentials—the bricks and mortar—of any systematic and successful rehearsing. Once this basic security is assured there quickly emerges a sense of proficiency and stability which, in their turn, permit style and character to underline a performance.

It cannot be too strongly reiterated that a systematic planning must underline all rehearsal.

Of all the many choir training sins it is the lack of projecting a sense of purpose which is unforgivable. How different the story when a choirmaster radiates enthusiasm, and has a genuine desire to communicate, to teach, and to produce a worthwhile end-product acceptable to the listener as an enrichment to worship.

This next section, a representative survey of anthems, service settings, hymns, psalms and responses, sets out to present a working approach to some of the technical and interpretative needs which would seem to characterise the styles found in the overall performance of church music by English composers. It embodies in a practical way the main headings discussed in Chapters 2 and 3.

1 In this part of the book, there is no attempt to provide an exhaustive or conclusive list, merely to present one's personal choice of eighteen examples which happen to span the main periods of English church music.

The restriction to examples of English music is, for these purposes, intentional.

What is analysed here is, broadly speaking, representative of the type of music to be found and used in the
average parish church repertoire.

2 The fact that the reference in each example is to a
specific edition in no way infers that other editions
should necessarily be dismissed as inferior, merely that
the edition in question is the one believed to be most
frequently in use. This does not apply to the anthems by
Loosemore, Redford, Purcell and Greene, where the
editions quoted are recommended as the most reliable in
terms of modern scholarship.

3 I hope that living composers who chance to see this book
will bear with my remarks about their music, even if they
may not necessarily agree with some of my suggestions
as to interpretation.

4 *The style of each piece, and how to interpret this, has
always been the uppermost consideration in my mind.*
Experience so often shows that some choirs have one
style and one type of tone, be the music by Byrd, Purcell,
Stanford or Britten. The fact that a choir sings with this
uniformity reflects the static approach of the choirmaster to the matter.

5 Although one would claim that the list which follows is a
reasonably representative one, it incidentally reflects the
fact that much church music is slow moving.

6 In adding a note for conductors I am not assuming, or
hoping, that every example will necessarily be conducted. This should not be the norm. These particular
comments are included for the sake of completeness and
to be helpful to those who need it.

7 Lastly, I cannot stress the difficulties of writing down
what would, and should, under normal conditions be
demonstrated practically. It would be so much easier to
explain this section verbally and to illustrate the various
points with the aid of a choir. This obviously could not

be, but I nevertheless hope the reader will be able to unravel—and comprehend—what I am trying to explain.

NOTE

Where recordings have been made these are quoted as information which may be of further help. As the performance of all music is a personalised matter and necessarily reflects how any one person envisages music—hence the word interpretation—some of my remarks may not be borne out by what is heard on a particular record. This is surely half the fun of music making and of comparing different performances.

O LORD, INCREASE MY FAITH

Henry Loosemore, edited by Watkins Shaw

Published by Novello in their Early
Church Music Series (No. 7).

Recording by King's College, Cambridge (RG 80), currently deleted from the catalogue.

This anthem was until recently believed to be by Orlando Gibbons. Subsequent evidence leaves little doubt but that Henry Loosemore, organist of King's College, Cambridge from 1627 to 1670, was in fact the composer.

On all counts, the edition by Watkins Shaw is to be recommended as authentic scholarship and preferable to the original Novello edition.

The construction of this small anthem is of much interest. The opening section (bars 1 to 6) makes its point through a harmonic scheme which helps to emphasise the deliberate mood of the text. The second section (bars 6 to 13) employs the contrast of imitative entries; these are simple but highly effective, with all four parts coming together at the end. The next part (bars 13 to 16), short though it may be, makes its point through the use of semiquavers which help to colour the idea of adversity. The final section, from bar 16 to the end, is in marked contrast and mirrors the beautiful text.

Although only twenty-five bars in all, the variety of 'figures' employed by the composer combine to make this intensely moving miniature one of the masterpieces of seventeenth-century English church music.

In terms of performance, much subtlety is needed. Each of the four sections should be approached in a different way with full scope being given to the interest in the part-writing. The editorial suggestions as to speed, dynamics and style are admirable and should be carefully adhered to.

Page 1

Bar 1   A slight crescendo on the first note will help the phrase to grow, with the $<\ >$ in the second bar further helping to emphasise the idea of the corporate nature of the text. The 'old' Novello edition employed the singular throughout. ('my faith'.)

Bar 2   In the soprano line, the comma after 'faith' is only minimal, but the stress on the beginning of 'strengthen' is important.

Bar 3   The bass note must be carefully tuned as a full semitone below the G♯ sung by the tenors in the previous bar.

Bar 4   The tenors must be sure to move down a whole tone from E to D, and then in bar 5 a further tone down to C.

Bar 6   While the alto C♯ must be a true major third, the C♮ which follows it must be fully flattened. It cannot be too firmly emphasised that in choral music, especially when unaccompanied, all accidentals must be treated with the greatest care, and tuned accordingly.

In this bar, and in bar 7, there will be no problem in accuracy of leads if each voice listens to the other.

Page 2

Bar 3   The tie on the first syllable of 'charity' must be firmly felt; this will avoid any hurrying of what is really a dotted note.

Bars 4 to 6 are relatively busy. Clarity of texture and diction will therefore help.

Page 3

Bars 1 and 2   Avoid the familiar tendency to turn the
♪♪♪ rhythm into a lazy triplet. Slightly leaning on
the first quaver will help to steady the rhythm and give
full value to the quaver. These groups should be sung
legato.

Bars 3 to 7   All the accidentals, being sharps, must be fully
tuned as upward semitones. Failure to do so could
result in a drop in pitch here.

Bar 6   The expression marks here need to be generously
interpreted.

Bar 7   As in bar 6 of the first page, so here the G♯ in the
alto must be fully flattened on the fourth beat.

Page 4

Bar 2   The tenor and bass entries here are not as easy as
they look. If the basses listen to the soprano A in the
first bar and the tenors the preceding alto note, this
should help. *The principle of finding your note from a
neighbouring part holds good for most contrapuntal
music.*

The basses in the final four bars must sing a true
legato; this applies particularly to the downward interval of a sixth.

Bar 5   The alto C♯, as the major third of the chord, must
be clear and true.

REJOICE IN THE LORD ALWAY

Anon. sixteenth century, once thought to have been composed by John Redford

Published by Oxford University Press (Tudor Church Music 55 revised).

Recordings by Bluecoat School (LPB 766)
               St Mary's, Warwick (LPB 654)
               St Michael's, Tenbury (ZRG 5423)
               Exultate Singers (VPS 1053)

This is best sung unaccompanied, though there is a school of thought which would opt, on grounds of scholarship, that most Tudor church music should be lightly accompanied on the organ.

The underlying mood here, dictated by the happy partnership of text and music, is that of a sparkling, fairly detached, and reasonably brisk two-in-a-bar, but with the minims generally more sustained than the crotchets and quavers.

The interval of a rising fourth, invariably moving from a weak to a strong word or syllable ('Re – JOICE' – 'let your SOFT – ness' and 'the LORD') is one of the characteristic and recurring trademarks here, as in so much English vocal music of this period.

This is further linked with a second unifying factor, the use of repeated notes which should invariably be detached and sung lightly, but with a rhythmic grip which counteracts any tendency to hurry.

and a – gain

Bar 5 The rhythmic stress in the soprano line can be either on the first or second notes:

'I say' or 'I SAY'

Bar 6 The sopranos must be unanimous in tidiness, ending 'oy–eece' exactly—and neatly—on the second minim.

What was said elsewhere concerning the arbitrary use of bar lines in music of this period is especially valid here. For example, in bar 12, where the first beat of the bar is on two unimportant words. The accents here are

In bars 21 to 25 the urgency of the repeated text and the nearness to each other of the vocal entries needs to be emphasised in such a way that the overall effect sounds busy.

As bar 25 ends the first complete section of the anthem, a certain licence needs to be taken so that the basses have time to breathe and are clearly heard commencing the new section in bar 26.

The mood and dynamics here change to a contrasted and sustained cantabile phrase. On no account must breath be taken in bar 28, bars 26 to 29 being one phrase. A slight crescendo on the dotted minim in bar 28 will help carry over the shape of the phrase.

The mood and dynamics change again in bar 33 where a firm tone of authority is needed. The descending stepwise crotchets ('is e'en at hand') should be sung lightly.

In bar 41, the soprano quavers must be as light as the proverbial feather. They will dance the more effectively if slightly detached, the slur under the four quavers indicating their being sung to one syllable and not to be confused with what otherwise would be a legato phrase.

In bar 44 the word 'prayer' should be thought of as a word of one syllable with the stress on the beginning.

In bars 46 to 50 the characteristic sixteenth-century underlay of the text must be used: 'pe – ti – see – ons'.

All four parts in bars 50 to 57 should aim at singing their phrases in one breath.

At bar 60 there should be a cut-off as in bar 25, and for the same reasons.

From here to the end, the mood is as reflective as the opening of the anthem was effervescent. The custom of settling for a slower tempo seems unnecessarily sentimental, the more so as most of the notes until the final Amen are almost exclusively crotchets and minims, which in themselves give the effect of a slower tempo. The phrases should be sung with a warmly glowing legato and shaped onwards and upwards to the high notes. This will help produce the musical, and therefore the dynamic, curves:

'And the peace of God which pass – eth'

From bar 78 to the end, a slight broadening of the tempo (now an obvious four-in-the-bar) will allow the florid lines to be musically shaped and without any hurrying, this the more so as the movement is by step. ATB have a wealth of linear interest here with each part needing to be shaped independently while building up to the apex (i.e. the highest notes) of its phrase. In this way the sum total of interest will be fully realised. The altos have the last say—at the end of the penultimate bar—while the major third (D) of the final chord should be slightly emphasised to give it, as with all major thirds of chords, the prominence needed.

CONDUCTOR

Although the music moves with a slight springiness at a steady two-in-a-bar, the normal idea of the first beat of the bar being rhythmically stressed does not always apply. A glance at bars 1 to 3 will show that the stresses occur on what would normally be the weak beat:

Re – joice	in the Lord	al – way
UP DOWN	UP DOWN	UP DOWN

The left hand can help in emphasising these accented words.

On the second line of page 3 it is best to have a slight comma at the end of bar one, otherwise the bass entry in bar two will be indistinct. The treatment of awkward corners such as this one and the final bar of page 5, depend on differing factors such as the size of the choir and the acoustics of the building. If, for example, there is an echo, the gap must be more clearly defined than in an acoustically dead church.

From this point on page 3 to the bottom of page 5, a more sustained beat will encourage the legato singing while allowing clarity for the crotchets on the bottom line of page 4 and the top of page 5.

On the bottom line of page 5 there must be a clearly indicated cut-off at the beginning of bar 4, both to guarantee the neatness of the final '-ks' and to ensure a new start, with a new mood, for the subsequent section. Although some conductors opt for a much slower four crotchets in the bar from here to the end, there seems little stylistic justification for this, although there will be some who would argue that the idea of peace should dictate a slow and soft situation.

From bar 3 of the second line of page 7 onwards, a definite four beats in the bar is desirable if the interest of the ATB part writing is to be given space to make itself felt. A reasonable rallentando is useful in the penultimate bar, so that there is plenty of space for the alto quavers (D and C).

THOU KNOWEST, LORD, THE SECRETS OF OUR
HEARTS
Henry Purcell, edited by Watkins Shaw
Published by Novello (Catalogue No. 29 0149 08)
Recordings by King's College, Cambridge (ASD 3316)
              St John's College, Cambridge (ZRG 724)

Bearing in mind the circumstances for which this pro-
foundly solemn piece of music was written, it will gain its
fullest effect in performance through a broad emphasis
based on the words. This will help produce the intensity
which was obviously in the composer's mind. Leaning on
the important words and syllables will also produce light
and shade as necessary features of the interpretation. This,
in its turn, will avoid a rigidly four-square sound which
could otherwise result.

Fundamentally then, it is the fusion of a slow tempo,
sustained phrases, and the almost larger than life stressing
of salient words and syllables. 'Thou *know–est, Lord*' etc.
The editor's direction 'Solemn, but expressive' would seem
to sum up what is needed.

The slow tempo, as in all slowly moving vocal music,
dictates a careful discipline in the matter of final consonants and their unanimity. Bar 3 is a case in point, where 'ts'
must be neatly and quickly articulated *on* the first beat of
bar 4 and *not* before or after that beat. Bars 11 and 19 have
similar features, while the word 'not' at the end of bar 4 is a
further example.

The rests throughout are an integral part of the full effect
of the scheme, both for punctuation and to emphasise even
further the solemnity of the mood. There must be no hurry-

ing in bars 5 and 6, nor at other places where single or repeated crotchets occur. All must be interpreted in a broad and expansive way.

In bar 7 the second syllable of 'prayer' needs to be sung lightly and at the last possible moment. The importance of the word 'most' (bars 10, 12 and 14) is obvious, while in 'holy' (bar 10), 'mighty' (bar 13), 'Saviour' (bar 15) and '-ternal' (bar 17), the crotchet must be carefully timed and lightly sung, as in each instance it carries the unimportant syllable. If, on each occasion, the dotted minim which precedes it is slightly emphasised, as it should always be, the crotchet will automatically shade it off.

In bars 21 to 23, the phrase 'for any pains of death' needs to be sustained with a warmly glowing and generous legato.

The first syllable of *Amen* is, despite the *poco rall.* commencing two bars previously, quicker than expected.

Although this is essentially a chordal anthem with the resulting melodic interest much to the fore, the full effect in performance relies heavily on the typically Purcellian harmonies. Accidentals, as in all vocal music, need treating with the greatest of respect, which means careful tuning, the more so here when they provide chromatic effects as in bass line of bar 6 and the soprano in bar 19.

The bass line throughout, whether loud or soft, calls for a firmly striding treatment.

Although the footnote on page 1 explains the absence of expression marks in the voice parts, it would obviously be helpful to the singers to pencil these in.

ORGAN

This is not an unaccompanied anthem. Although the suggested organ part doubles the voices, it also provides a necessary contrast in texture which should be borne out in the registration. For example, the use of an oboe stop from bar 18 to the end could help reinforce, even colour, the text at this point.

CONDUCTOR

A broad, generous, and smoothly sustained beat can be a very helpful 'extra' in music such as this, the more so if the minim rests are clearly indicated and given full value.

A fairly big and flowing legato beat will help to intensify the drama of this particular anthem which, as with so much church music, looks deceptively easy on paper but in performance is more than deceptively demanding.

JESU, JOY OF MAN'S DESIRING

J. S. Bach, edited by H. P. Allen

Published by Oxford University Press (Church Music Society Reprint No. 16 A)

Recordings by London Bach Society (EXP 2)
Liverpool Cathedral (LPB 779)

Although this edition provides for two verses, it is usual to sing only the first verse, otherwise the anthem can become unduly long and repetitive.

The singers must not only follow the organ interludes but establish in their minds both the pulse and the rhythm so that when they commence singing each new phrase they will be able to do so at the exact tempo. This is even more essential at the start as the triplet rhythm in the accompaniment ceases when the voices enter. Choirs are notorious at 'switching off' during the organ interludes in an anthem such as this one.

In all choral music the pulse must be felt throughout, whether or not the choir are actually singing.

The parallel is the human heart beat which continues to function whether we are awake or asleep.

The singing should always be legato and sustained, yet flowing. It will thus contrast in mood with the distinctive character of the accompaniment. The curve in dynamics in almost every phrase should be

Page 1

Bar 9   A comma as such after the word 'Jesu' merely
        produces a hiccup. The effect of a comma will be felt
        by shading off the second syllable and stressing 'joy'.

Page 2

Bar 6   In the first beat of the soprano part the secret is to
        lean on the quaver. This will help to ensure it being
        given *full* value. Otherwise the tendency will be to
        shorten it so that ♪♫ resembles a distorted trip-
        let.

Bar 7   There must be two full beats on 'bright'; this means
        that the final consonant will be sounded *on* the third
        beat, not before.

Page 3

Bar 8   The verbal stress here is '*pyr* – ring'

Page 4

Bar 2   The sopranos' rhythm on the second and third
        beats is a trap with the crotchets on B and A easily
        confused with the identical bar on page 7 where there
        is merely a minim on an A. The unwary allow their
        concentration to relax at the end of the phrase so that
        they are caught out just when they think they are home
        and dry.

Page 5

Bar 2   The basses must concentrate on the C♮ which
        comes after a prominent C♯ in the organ part at the
        end of the previous bar. Having thus modulated to the
        key of D, the basses immediately cancel this out by

flattening their C. The alto note on the third beat (G♯) must be fully sharpened, while in the third bar the tenors and basses must carefully tune their F♮. In this bar, the upward leap of an octave in the bass must be approached as lightly as the downward quavers which follow.

Page 6

Bar 1   The rhythm in the soprano line needs care. The tie must be 'felt' and will be made the easier if the singers listen to the altos and basses on the second beat, after which the two semiquavers will be legato and un-hurried.

Bar 2   The tenor E needs slightly emphasising as the major third of the chord.

Page 7

Bars 1 and 2   The accents are on the first syllable of each word. This will avoid 'soar – *ring*, dy – *ying*'. The comma in the first bar can then be dispensed with.

Bar 4   Is a full three beats.

ORGAN

Although the left hand (Manual II) is written as ♪♩ it is always played as a triplet rhythm ♩♪ coinciding with the right-hand triplets.

A light and flowing sound is called for, almost dancing but always legato. Any semblance of a rallentando must be avoided at the end of each of the interludes.

Registration, which remains the same throughout, should be determined by balancing the oboe solo with the accompaniment of Manual II. If there is no oboe on the organ, a Great flute might be used, accompanied by a softer stop on the Swell.

For a one manual organ it is not difficult to re-arrange the
notes where the parts cross. If, as in bar 8 of page 1, the
accompaniment goes over the top of the tune, the high
notes must be omitted so as to allow the tune to stand out.

This applies especially in such places as the second line of
page 7. Even with a two manual organ, it may be impossible
to play neatly all the notes in the left hand, in which case
any of the lower notes, printed in small type, which provide
too wide a stretch, should be omitted.

CONDUCTOR

Little more than an unobtrusive legato beat is needed here.
It is useful if the left hand helps in emphasising the important words and syllables: 'Je – su, joy of man's de – sir –
ing'. The conductor can also help in preparing the way for
the voice parts to enter after each of the organ interludes.
This provides an added safeguard while increasing the confidence which allows the singers to concentrate first and
foremost on musical matters.

THOU VISITEST THE EARTH
Maurice Greene edited by Francis Jackson
Published by Novello (Early Church Music Series No. 13)

This chestnut is so well known as to be an instance of familiarity, if not exactly breeding contempt, more than likely to breed carelessness in performance. How often one hears the repeated ♪ ♪ rhythm getting faster and slacker until the figure becomes an out of shape triplet with the music losing most of its eighteenth-century grace and character.

Here is an instance where it is certainly best to forget the familiar 'old' Novello edition (which for many choirs is the only version they know) and start afresh with this new edition, determined to sing it correctly and perform it for what it is, a beautiful dance tune of its time, underlined by an enviable and precise gracefulness.

The solo passage (pages 1 and 2) can be sung either by a tenor or by the trebles (or sopranos) in unison.

The style in which this anthem should be sung is a most important and fundamental consideration.

The recurring dotted figure must *always* be light and dancing, the more so as the anthem progresses and this figure becomes the more familiar and repetitive. It will help if the dotted quaver is almost double dotted, as was the eighteenth-century custom. The B♮ in bar 13 is similarly the more effective if made into a semiquaver, as editorially suggested, with the note preceding it double dotted.

By contrast, all the long notes need to have a sense of growing, this being obtained through a slight crescendo on to the next note, such as a string player would automatically do.

The editorial suggestions printed above bars 5 and 6 are delightful stylistic considerations which legitimately improve the original, while the trills in bars 7 and 8 are examples of typical eighteenth-century ornamentation. These features recur later in the anthem.

There should obviously be a rall. to broaden out the final two bars of the anthem, otherwise the ending will be very abrupt.

ORGAN

The pedals should not be used. What was said about the length of dotted notes in the voice parts applies equally to the organ part from which at the outset the singers take their cue.

The expression marks editorially included in the voice parts should be mirrored by the organ, so producing balance and contrast.

Finally, do read Dr Jackson's 'Editorial Procedure' set out on the front inside cover. It contains some helpful information for all concerned.

CONDUCTOR

All that is needed is a simple and unaffected beat, but one which will relay the underlying lilt of the music. This can best be achieved through a slight emphasis on the first beat of each bar, offset by a light and almost springy second and third beat.

MAGNIFICAT AND NUNC DIMITTIS IN D MINOR
Walmisley
Published by Novello
Recording by St John's College, Cambridge (ZK 3)

This remarkable piece of music was anything but a child of its time. With its independent organ part, the disposition of the voices, and separate Glorias for each canticle, it stands out head and shoulders above the almost uniformly stereotyped profusion of settings which are its contemporary.

Its significance, both in relation to the paucity of invention of much which immediately preceded it and what it led the way to in terms of S. S. Wesley and Stanford, is therefore the more remarkable. It is useful to read what E. H. Fellowes has to say about this service in *English Cathedral Music*, also Kenneth Long in *The Music of the English Church* (pages 356 and 357).

With all these considerations in mind, it is regrettable that the familiarity of the music reduces many a performance to a mundane sing-through which is often devoid of much in the way of thought or vision. As with all familiar church music, a searchingly critical new look can reveal much.

MAGNIFICAT

The general plan is an alternation between a broad TB unison and a much gentler SSA verse treatment which calls for a careful balance between the three voices. This makes for an interesting and not irrelevant comparison to the way in which the Tudor composers contrasted their 'verse' and 'full' writing.

A generation ago the unison TB sections would, we are
told, have frequently sounded remarkably like the 'roaring
bulls of Bashan'. This approach still fitfully lingers on in
some circumstances. But—from the outset, the conception
is far more subtle than that, even if we only remember that the
music moves at two minims in the bar, *not* four crotchets.

Page 2

The initial phrase, although twice broken by rests, is in fact
the entire page. It is an apex governed by the high notes, the
rests in bars 6 and 10 merely serving as breathing, or
punctuation, spaces.

The crotchets and the ♩ ♪ figure must be treated as
dancing rhythms, especially when, as at 'spirit hath
rejoiced', the notes are repeated.

Page 3

By a marked contrast, the SSA verse should be a sustained
legato and quieter in mood. There is certainly no breath
after 'regarded', while the comma after the first 'lowliness'
is merely a brief mark of punctuation to help in reiterating
the words. At the end of the second line, the phrasing
should be '*hence*–forth'.

Page 4

The unison on the top line relies on a weighty breadth of
tone to sustain the full impact of this fine phrase, the notes
of which could hardly be simpler.

In line 2 it should be '*ho*–li' and not 'ho–*lee*', while on the
bottom line care must be taken to ensure that the B♮ in the
second soprano is a full semitone up from the preceding B♭.

Page 5

The crotchets in bars 2 and 3 should be underlined by a

firmly sustained legato, with the 1st sopranos slightly strengthening in tone their held D.

'He hath shewed strength with His arm' is obviously one phrase which will be helped as such by a slight crescendo on 'strength'.

At the end of the 2nd line the quaver on 'in' is a very quick note to be sung by all voices as near as possible to the second minim beat. This applies especially to the sopranos and altos entering after four bars' rest, and for whom this could easily sound lethargic. In bar 6 of the bottom line, the second sopranos must carefully and fully flatten the preceding F♯.

Page 6

Similarly, the alto C♯ at the beginning of the second line must be fully sharpened to produce the major 3rd of the chord, only to be immediately flattened again in the next bar.

All such chromatic notes must be carefully tuned as accurate semitones, the more so when they change so quickly.

The bottom line, as the tenors' and basses' last big moment, should have a real sense of culmination and climax, not least in the organ part.

Page 7

This can be sung either as directed or without repeat, in either instance by the full choir alternating with a smaller group. The prevailing mood is gentle with the long sustained phrases contrasting in no uncertain way with the forcibility of what went immediately before and what follows this section. Although the melodic interest here is obvious, this must extend to the altos, tenors and basses, especially in places such as the touch of colour provided by the tenors in the two final bars.

Page 8

Avoid what could so easily be an accent in bar 2. Apart from the first syllable of 'glory' and 'Father' all the words are relatively unimportant and should therefore be sung lightly. In the second line there must be three full beats on 'Ghost' with the final 'st' sounding quickly and neatly *on* the fourth beat.

From here to the end it is gloriously flowing lines, generously vocal and full of interest. Even so, the basses must resist any eleventh hour temptation to become 'bulls of Bashan', however temporarily. If sung lightly, but with resonance, the top Cs and Ds can be memorable.

It is best if the final line is in strict time apart from a slight broadening out on the penultimate minims in the alto and tenor line. On the final chord, the alto F♯, as the third of the now major chord, needs to glow with warmth and with slight emphasis.

NUNC DIMITTIS

Although marginally slower than Magnificat it still moves at two-in-a-bar with the general treatment much the same as in Magnificat. The notion that the Nunc Dimittis should always be soft and slow is an old wives' tale. The words are anything but funereal.

Page 10

The long notes in the first phrase need to grow in tone and intensity. If the first word is tonally static for four beats it will sound very dull.

Good singers will emulate string players who invariably make long notes grow in tone through to the next note. This calls for concentration and control but the end product will be artistic.

In line 2 the natural phrasing will be
    'ac – *cord* – ing to thy *word*'

Page 11

Bars 3 to 11 must never be hammered out but sung lightly so that they dance.

Gloria should be a broad sound but with rather more edge on the tone. Every crotchet, either singly or in pairs, should be unhurried and expansive.

Page 12

In the top line avoid the all too easy trap of a rigid accentuation which will produce

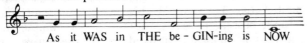

As it WAS in THE be - GIN-ing is NOW

As the words here are a statement of fact, no undue accentuation is called for anywhere.

The general mood of this page is in many respects identical with that of the latter part of the Magnificat Gloria. The pause preceding the final Amen is best if thought of as a strict three minims followed by a full minim rest for breath before the final *soft* Amen where the tenors have an important role, the major 3rd once again.

ORGAN

MAGNIFICAT

A combination of a broad legato with the essential two-in-a-bar mentioned earlier will, from the outset, help to produce the spacious mood which underlines the character of the music. To this end, no crotchet or quaver must ever be hurried if this highly personalised organ part is to sound expansive.

Two contrasted sets of stops are needed, adapted as necessary to the resources of the instrument:
1. Great to Principal plus full, or nearly full, Swell.
2. Choir flutes (8ft and 4ft) *or* the parallel on the Great.

Page 2

The initial pedal note, which is not merely a thump, is the more emphatic if it is slightly shortened and used as a springboard before the first phrase proper which coincides with the voice parts.

The pedal throughout must always be played at the written pitch, and not an octave lower.

Page 4

Bars 1 to 3 are a most effective contrast if left unaccompanied. As bars 3 to 5 employ a big stretch in the right hand, it is in the best interests of clarity for the left hand to play the lower note of each right-hand chord. Alternatively, in the third and fourth chords, the lower notes of the right hand (A and D), which appear elsewhere in these chords, can be omitted.

The diminuendo at the end of the top line must be carefully graded by reducing the registration just *before* the final chord (not with it) and similarly, before the first two chords of the second line.

All stops changes should be effected in that split second just before a new chord, never when the chord is sounding.

Line 2, as a moving part with passing notes, must be clearly articulated. This will help the singers to 'feel' the rhythm on their unison Fs.

As the 'Sw. Reed' direction on the final chord of this page heralds a tame solo, it can easily be dispensed with as such, probably to advantage. In any event, a trumpet or horn is needed here, an oboe being ineffective.

Page 5

In the section commencing at bar 4, the right hand should be slightly detached so as to emphasise both the rhythm and the forcefulness of what is being sung. A re-arrangement of notes similar to the top line of page 4 will probably be helpful.

Page 6

The bottom line marks a big tonal climax, the biggest sound so far. A slight allargando in the final three bars will make this the more impressive.

Page 7

If this is to be sung twice, it should preferably be unaccompanied the second time. If the organ is used, it must always be a light and unobtrusive sound. Gloria calls for a treatment similar to the previous loud sections.

NUNC DIMITTIS

If there is no conductor, the choir must look across at each other and come in as soon as possible on hearing the organ chord. After this the organist sets the pace. He must therefore think this out carefully, beforehand and during the Second Lesson, so that the correct tempo is established from the outset.

Until the top of page 11 it is probably best to play on the Swell, with pedal.

Page 10

The crescendo at the end of line 2 is minimal and relies on the choir more than the organ. Opening the swell box achieves what is needed here.

Page 11

Bar 3 onwards calls for a new set of stops, something such as Choir 8ft or 8ft and 4ft.

For Gloria, the direction 'Full to 15th' and, on page12,

86

'Sesq. and Mixt' will probably have to be adapted to the comparative resources of many instruments. Even so, page 12 should be louder than page 11, with the chords divided between the hands as suggested previously.

Page 12

The pause on the bottom line is best made into three minims followed by a minim rest and a soft final Amen.

CONDUCTOR

A broad and expansive beat is called for in the robust sections, with a less vigorous, though no less rhythmic, approach to the contrasted SSA passages.

The minim note or chord which prefaces each section needs a clear and confident downbeat which will act as a springboard for the singers.

The nature of page 7 dictates a gentler and more sustained beat.

At the end of page 9 the whole bar rest should be clearly indicated so that there can be an assured attack on the final Amen.

At the start of Nunc Dimittis, the beat must be clear and rhythmic if choir and organist are to respond in establishing the pulse.

What was said in relation to the singers about the pause before the final Amen is even more relevant to the conductor.

FROM THE RISING OF THE SUN

Ouseley

Published by Novello

Recording by St Michael's College, Tenbury (ZRG 5423)

This is music typical of so much of its period, music which can so easily sound so routine, uneventful and repetitive. Yet it contains many subtleties which will transform mere notes into something thoroughly attractive. Nor is it all that difficult to give it a face-lift, provided all concerned in its performance really wish to take some trouble and exercise a little imagination.

A surfeit of semibreves and minims always tends to give a visual impression which inevitably seems to suggest slow plodding. If the music were written in $\frac{4}{4}$ rather than $\frac{4}{2}$ a lot of the problems, most of which are probably figments of the imagination, would soon disappear.

Even as written, a start will at least be made if we *think* in terms of two-in-a-bar instead of four, even though this may not work out all the way. Although there is no metronome mark or other indication of suggested tempo, *moderato* or a shade faster would seem to be a sensible pace.

Page 1

The first four bars set a pattern which will also apply to much which follows. If we abandon the normal idea of four-in-a-bar accentuation (*ONE*, two, *three*, four) in favour of a form of speech rhythm, there is a subtle transformation from a rigidly

'From the | RI – sing of the | SUN un – to the |

GO – ing down of the | SAME'

into a musical flexibility:

'From the | RI – sing of the | SUN unto the going

down of the same'

the more so if all the words except those marked with an asterisk are sung lightly.

A gradual increase in dynamics from the beginning through to the third beat of bar 3, with a corresponding diminuendo to the first beat of bar 5, will further relay the idea of phrase shape. The upward octave which the basses have to negotiate in bar 3 must be sung lightly and without drawing attention to itself.

The second phrase (bars 5 to 9) make their point through a more obviously marked rhythm and a definite change of mood. The positive text ('*shall* be great', not 'maybe will be great') is the further enhanced by the change in dynamics and the simple expedient of the altos and basses reiterating the soprano and tenor lead a bar later. Already, within the first eight bars, there are subtleties of mood and interpretation which can quickly transform mere notes into living music.

Page 2

In order to see through the long phrase in the second line, there must be no break or comma after 'place' nor similarly after 'name' in the first bar of the bottom line.

The alto in bar 3 of the second line should be sung lightly; these two notes are no excuse for a solo, however short lived!

The end of the second line begins a cumulative build-up through a change of mood in the words. This continues through to the pause in the second line of page 3 by which time, and not before, the choir should be singing ff. A broadening out of tempo in the first three bars of the second line helps to heighten the climax and the authority of the words, the more so if this is sung both rhythmically and slightly detached.

Pages 3 and 4

For the rest, it is the same as the beginning until the third bar of the second line of page 4 which can be a trap for the unwary, especially the exposed soprano line.

Page 4

The final three bars of the anthem sum it all up and must be sung with considerable emphasis (which does not mean fff), but with the interest in the alto and tenor lines fully high-lighted, not least the flattened 7th (D♭) in the tenor.

ORGAN

The anthem is probably best when sung without accompaniment. If, however, the choir are to be supported, the organ should be softer than the singing, while some transposing of the voice parts will add a touch of independent melodic interest, as in all good continuo playing. Merely to copy the voice parts note by note is unimaginative.

The preliminary 'doorknocker' at the start, and again halfway through page 3, is meaningless. It draws attention to itself and there is every reason to dispense with it.

CONDUCTOR

A minimum of gesture is all that is needed here. The beat should obviously be rhythmic, light, and perhaps slightly springy, but more assertive in the loud passages. A conductor can be especially helpful in the climax on page 3 and again at the end of the anthem.

BLESSED BE THE GOD AND FATHER

S. S. Wesley

Of the two editions currently in use, what follows relates to
that published by Novello (Octavo anthems No. 15)

Recordings by Hereford Cathedral (LRLI 5126)
St John's College, Cambridge (ZK 3)
Leeds Parish Church (LPB 686)
Liverpool Cathedral (LPB 779)

Page 1

The opening section calls for a calculated discipline. As a
statement of fact, it relies on a complete unanimity of
rhythmic movement between the four parts. This is the
more impressive when linked to a careful tonal balance in
which the melodic context is supported, though never in
any way dominated by ATB.

Ideally, breath should only be taken at rests. This will
help in the onward movement of the long phrases.
Although the final ten bars of this section are one complete
phrase, they cannot be sung in one breath. Some faking is
therefore needed. If individual singers take breath as and
when they need to, it will produce the effect of one long
phrase, provided it is agreed who takes breath and where.

In bar 2, as elsewhere when long notes occur in the
middle of a phrase, a slight crescendo will help in carrying
through the phrase shape.

In bar 7, the crotchet rest is best thought of as a mark of
punctuation, the final syllable of 'which' being sounded on
the third beat, and not before.

In bar 4 of the 2nd line the natural stress must be
observed—'mer – cy' not 'mer –cy'.

Bar 6 of the bottom line is virtually speech rhythm while maintaining a sustained phrase. A slight rubato in all four parts will help, whereas a rigid interpretation of the written note values will sound four-square and unsatisfactory.

Page 2

The crescendo begins in the second half of bar 2, not before, and continues to grow consistently until the *end* of the word 'dead', the final consonant of which sounds on the first beat of the next bar.

The high notes for tenor and bass, if allowed to be unduly enthusiastic, will predominate and obscure both the balance and the emphasis of the soprano line. The build up of tone and the directional shape of each part is a special effect mirroring admirably the idea of resurrection.

The next section is virtually a continuation in unison of the tempo and mood of what has gone before. If the altos sing here it must be in the tenor or bass register, not alto as such.

This recit. demands a poised tone, never being allowed to approach anything remotely laboured or lugubrious, and this taking into account the wide compass between the highest and lowest notes. Due emphasis must be given to long notes and to the triplet on the bottom line. *There is always a tendency to hurry triplets* which are best thought of as being lethargic, expansive, even deliberately drawn out.

'Ready' at the end of page 2 marks the start of a quick crescendo heightened by the almost electric urgency of the text and the high notes.

Page 3

How the soprano section from here until page 5 is sung will be determined by the available forces. If there is no suitable solo voice a small group, or even all the sopranos, must

suffice. The passage beginning at the fourth line needs
some form of contrast to produce the antiphonal effects
necessary here. It will also prepare the way for the divided
soprano line on the top of page 5.

As the singers are naturally anxious to come in correctly
after the florid organ interlude at the top of page 3, the first
word ('but') is sometimes subjected to a thunp and is
accented out of all proportion. Being a relatively unimportant word, it should be sung quietly with a slight crescendo
through to 'He' and then on to 'called'.

In line 2, bar 6, 'manner' should be sung as one would say
it, lightly, legato and with no hint of an accent on the
syncopation. In line 3, bars 2–6 are one phrase and must be
sung as such, after which the repetition of 'in fear' increases
the intensity, the more so if the 'r' of 'fear' is very slightly
rolled. The rit. in bar 6 of line 4 is followed by a new and
faster tempo, ♩ = 104 being rather more brisk than the
Moderato to which Wesley equated it.

This new tempo will immediately be established if singers and organist listen to each other. The clue is the quaver
movement in the organ part.

In this section each phrase, usually of four bars, must, if
the musical curve is to be convincing, be sung in one breath.
Thus, in the first two phrases, the natural rise and fall of the
notes, together with an equally natural emphasis on the
words, will combine to dictate musically satisfying sounds.

Two further points here:
1. 'pure' = 'pee–ure', not 'poor'.
2. 'that ye', not 'tha–*chee*'.

Page 4

The chromatic notes, F♯, C♯, and D♭ need very careful
tuning to ensure they are accurate rising semitones. A slight
increase in energy preceding an upward interval will help
produce an accurate interval and not one that is slightly
short measure. A useful parallel is the extra energy needed

on the accelerator when driving a car up a steep incline. For example, in line 3:

a   pure

Page 5

Careful tuning is needed for the divided sopranos singing in thirds, especially those notes which produce the third of the chord.

For the recit. (lines 3 to 5) the direction *ad lib* must not be taken literally. The speech rhythm which must govern matters here will be helped if the phrases are first said, then sung.

There are three main sections, each ending with a pause:

Section one
1 Some emphasis is called for on 'not' which should be made a full crotchet.
2 'rup–ti–ble' (bar 1) is best sung as a triplet.
3 No comma or breath after 'seed'.
4 'but of incorruptible, by the word of God' should, by contrast, be in strict time, helped by the minim movement in the organ part.
5 The pause on 'God' should equal four crotchets.

Section two
1 The first two notes, even if they are low B♭s, must not be allowed to growl. If they are light and detached they will lead on with ease to 'flesh'.
2 'glory of man' needs careful tuning, especially the C♮ which must be fully flattened.
3 'flower' is two syllables.
4 The pause on 'grass' becomes rhythmic if it is given

three crotchet beats, followed by an equally rhythmic quaver rest and 'The'.

Section three

1 This should be no slower than the preceding passages and should be sung in reasonably strict time.

2 Nor must 'withereth' be hurried. It is a further example of deliberate speech rhythm.

3 The final note is C *or* F—not both—with a preference for the former.

Page 6

The new tempo here is Allegretto, with all that implies in terms of a sophisticated dance-like chorus.

Remembering that the pulse here is *two minims*, the rest on the first beat is a springboard:

(one)   *BUT*

A tightly dotted rhythm is needed with all dots given full value. The repetition of this phrase should both reiterate and heighten the dramatic effect.

For the imitative entries beginning at the bottom of the page, a springy and rhythmic style is called for:

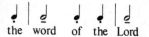

the word of the Lord

Page 7

The tenor lead will need care in helping to establish the C minor tonality which emerges here.

In line 2, the soprano E♭ (bar 1) and E♮ (bar 3) will need similar care, not least the E♮ which is unexpected and quickly cancelled by a further E♭ in bar 4.

Care must also be taken over the dotted rhythm in the soprano in bar 4 where the dot must be given *full* value.

Throughout this page, accidentals shifting the key centre must be accurately tuned.

Page 8

The bass line throughout this page needs careful concentration, not least the chromatic notes in bars 4 to 9, similarly the alto in bars 5 to 7.

In the final line all parts, especially the basses, must sing in strict time with the tenors paying particular attention to the diminished 5th (G to D♭).

The pauses on the final Amen are most effective if sung in strict time, with four minims on each note.

ORGAN

The first section being unaccompanied, some form of introduction is needed. A mere chord of E♮ is a partial answer whereas the first six bars, played in exactly the same time as that in which the beginning of the anthem is to be sung, will help establish key and time for the singers. This also creates a more artistic prelude than a mere chord.

Page 2

The organ in bars 5 to 7 must provide an impressive support for the voices. The full swell effect will be heightened through opening the swell box as suggested. If the pedals are omitted here, the effect is immediately heightened by their appearance in the next line where the organ tone, based on Great diapasons, changes to a broadly sustained legato which should spaciously underline page 2.

Page 3

The miniature flourish written in small notes in bar 5 is best played as a semiquaver triplet. The addition of a soft Swell reed in bar 2 of the third line, backed up by a gradual Swell box crescendo through to bar 6, will ensure useful colour and support to the voices similarly making their own crescendo through the shape of the phrase.

The new tempo commencing in bar 7 of the fourth line *must* be set by the organist whose quavers, if they are neat and rhythmic, will leave the singers no room for any doubt about what is happening. As moving inner parts, the quavers must be clearly and confidently articulated.

A light pedal should be used throughout this section.

Page 5

In the fourth bar of line 2 the organ must clearly indicate the slight easing of tempo needed here so that the three final quavers of the bar lead easily on to the contrasted sound and mood which dictates the recit. commencing on line 3.

On the bottom line, the minim and crotchet movement will, if rhythmically and clearly articulated, be a considerable guideline for the singers. Some re-allocating and thinning out of notes will probably be necessary here, the composer having written unduly complicated chords in each hand. The final chord of this page gains in its impact if it is separated from the previous section by the addition of a crotchet rest.

As a highly dramatic moment achieved through very simple means, this big chord can, within reason, be as long and as loud as one dares to make it. By doing this, it becomes even more a stroke of genius.

Page 6

The semiquaver at the end of bar 5 and again in the first bar of the bottom line will be the more rhythmically clear if slightly lengthened and separated from the chord which follows. These big chords make their impact by being bold and assertive; their effect will be the more heightened if the right hand is detached (marcato) while the left hand and pedals are legato.

From the bass entry in the bottom line onwards, registration should be reduced to a bright and sparkling sound, with Great to Fifteenth, or its equivalent, being the point of departure.

Page 7

Further stops can be added on the fourth beat of the third bar of the bottom line, thus marking the start of the final main section.

Page 8

As with the voice parts, the organ must maintain strict time through to the end, with the final three chords neatly in time and preferably detached from each other for clarity.

CONDUCTOR

Page 1

Because of the dot at the beginning of the anthem, the second beat of the first bar must be clearly defined. All rests must be equally clearly marked and not hurried.

Page 2

The join at the end of the top line must be emphasised, *and in strict time*. As the recit. proceeds the beat can, with good effect, become two-in-a-bar rather than four.

Page 3

The start of the soprano solo on the second beat of bar 5 is a difficult corner. It will be made the easier by a clear down beat followed by an equally clear second and third beat. In line 4 the conductor can help the organist to establish the new tempo in bar 7. Between them they can make the new speed abundantly clear from the outset.

Page 4

As this section continues, it will help the flow of the music if the beat becomes more two-in-a-bar rather than four.

Page 5

For the recit. (lines 3 to 5) the main accents, and little else, need to be marked as a series of downbeats. For example, in line 4

'For all <u>flesh</u> is as <u>grass</u>, and all the <u>glo</u> – ry of <u>man</u>

as the <u>flower</u> of <u>grass</u>'.

Page 6

A smallish, springy, and highly rhythmic beat is all that is needed here to project the sparkle of this essentially two-in-a-bar chorus. For the bottom of the page and the top of page 7 it will help if the leads are indicated to the singers concerned.

Page 8

This should be in strict time with the rhythmic 'spring' neat and precise and with no slackening of the tempo through to the last note. As was mentioned earlier, each pause at the end should be four strict beats.

JESU, THE VERY THOUGHT OF THEE
Edward C. Bairstow
Published by Oxford University Press (A5 S.A.T.B.)
Recording by York Minster (CNN 4977)

Here is music relying for its full impact on sustained singing
with each and every expression makr exploited to the full.
This means a succession of extended crescendos and
diminuendos which must be carefully controlled and measured out, for it is always so much easier to $\diagup$ than to
$\diagdown$ especially, as here, in fairly slow moving music.

Even so, it is the cultivating of disciplines such as these
which help to single out the best in choral techniques. In
this particular instance it allows the phrases to unfold with
the sense of occasion for which Bairstow was renowned, for
he was a master of choral sound—and of how to relate it to
the liturgy.

Having emphasised the expressive qualities of this short
anthem, chording and blend are no less important factors in
relaying the texture of the music. This includes knowing
when you have a tune and when to keep your distance in
favour of some other part.

It all ultimately depends on that basic must of all con-
certed music making, the need for everyone to listen to
everyone else so that each and every phrase becomes
packed out with interest and colour. This is surely what
music is all about.

In the initial stages of learning the notes some discreet,
but not necessarily continuous, help from the keyboard will
increase confidence.

Here also, as in all vocal music moving at a slow tempo,

diction needs care. This applies especially to the more explosive final consonants as in 'sweetness', 'breast', and 'rest' which can so easily draw undue attention to themselves through being too prolonged, and consequently ragged.

Page 1

Looking at the music in some detail, the $<$ $>$ on the first syllable of 'Jesu', especially in the soprano and bass lines, needs an immediate crescendo through to the third beat and then an equally controlled diminuendo through to the beginning of the next bar.

This is harder to achieve than it would at first seem, either individually or as a group. The same applies to the alto and tenor entries, notably the alto which has the moving interest.

This immediate warming of the tone is a necessary artistic point; it bears out the universal need for any long note to grow or diminish in its intensity, never to stay still.

The upward interval of a sixth is a distinctive feature of the first page. The sixth, especially when major, is always a strong and prominent interval which demands careful tuning, the distance being such that there is the risk of it being given short measure. It is always helpful to think of upward intervals, and approach them, as a direct leap from point A to point B. It is the unethical sliding up to the high note which causes inaccuracies in tuning:

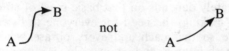

While *pp* is the composer's warning against over-enthusiasm in approaching the upward intervals, *ten.* is a valid encouragement to slightly linger on the word 'thought'. These are subtle points which will be rewarded in no small measure through careful rehearsal.

Page 2

In bar 3 ATB must bring out the maximum melodic and textual interest which is supported here by the sustained soprano note and the upward moving bass. This bar begins the cumulative crescendo which builds up in intensity to the top line of the next page.

In bar 6 it is better if the sopranos take no breath after 'breast'. By singing the bottom line in one breath any untidiness on the final 'st' will be avoided. Try it both ways and you will soon see the difference. If the expression marks in this bar are implemented, the mood of this new section will be clearly defined. There will also be no problems over ATB finding their entries if all concerned take their cue in turn from the soprano lead.

Page 3

Bar 2. While the soprano line here must be sustained, and reinforced through to the fortissimo climax, the interest of the high tenor phrase should slightly predominate. This is then carried through into the next line where, although there is a general $\diagup\diagdown$ the alto and bass should retain the interest of their moving parts and diminuendo slightly later than the sopranos and tenors.

Choirs are notoriously bad at turning pages too late and consequently not being ready, as the tenors must be here, for the distinctive B♮ on the top of page 4.

Page 4

In bar 2 the interest in the alto line must slightly predominate, with the D fully flattened. In bar 3 the sopranos must watch the conductor while thinking, and moving, as one on the F at the 3rd beat. Liaison between singers and conductor, and this includes the choir carefully and accurately counting the rests in bars 3 and 4, will ensure a confident security from the outset of the final nine bars.

Here, because of the longer note values, the quiet singing and the positioning of the D♮s and D♭s, pitch could suffer. The last line must certainly be sung lightly, almost in the head voice. SAT must focus attention on the bass line during the final five bars. Each part is dependent on the other here.

The comma before the final word implies a distinct, if short, gap which serves to emphasise the word 'rest'. *ppp* is *very* soft, while the final 'st', which comes on the cut-off, must be quickly enunciated and unobtrusive, but it must be heard. If there is any doubt about how to divide the basses, more singers should be on the bottom E♭ than on the top note.

CONDUCTOR

A conductor is essential here. The slowish pulse, long phrases and preponderance of quiet singing combine to demand the need for an overall direction. Otherwise, left to their own devices, the singers are almost certain to get slower, the impetus will flag and a general uneasiness prevail.

Through gesture and systematic rehearsal, a good conductor will encourage his singers towards each and every expression mark and in the general unfolding and growing of the phrases. He will also note that *Andante tranquillo* is not *Adagio*, and that there is no rallentando marked at the end, the longer notes providing the feeling of the music coming to a close.

Here, as throughout the anthem, the wise conductor will breathe with his singers; he will also mentally phrase and help project the shape of the music, pinpointing to his singers through his eyes and hands exactly what he—and the music—require.

On page 4 the conductor must look at the sopranos and clearly indicate the F which comes on the third beat of the 3rd bar. The rests here and in the next bar need only a very small flick of the finger with, as a safeguard, the singers watching. What is important is the third beat of bar 4 which is the preparation for the singers' entry on the next beat.

For the final five bars of the anthem, the conductor must concentrate on the basses, and they on him. He must give a clear and unmistakably broad third beat, while also giving SAT an equally clear down beat at the commencement of each bar. A neat cut-off is essential at the comma before the final chord.

This is the type of anthem in which many a choir may do little more than sing the correct notes. A sensitive conductor will make the notes and phrases come alive so that the music unfolds in a colourful and convincing way. Such is the power of the conductor.

ORGAN

At the start, a triad of E♭   rather than a single

B♭, will more readily help the singers to establish the tonality in their minds.

GOD IS GONE UP

Gerald Finzi

Published by Boosey and Hawkes (C.C.S. 39)

Recordings by Peterborough Cathedral (LPB 658)
            Gloucester Cathedral (LPB 783)
            Exeter Cathedral (Excath 1) obtainable
            only from Exeter Cathedral

This dramatic and colourful anthem is finely constructed.
By exploiting to the full what is in every respect a superb
text, the composer contrived to build two boldly declama-
tory sections around a contrasted and beautifully lyrical
middle section. The result is a highly charged score underlined by a sense of occasion in which the big moments
project excitement and impact.

Although the composer's directions are marked *Allegro
(non troppo) maestoso*, the metronome marking, at ♩=
138, indicates a livelier speed. Whether or not there is a
conductor, the singers must always be ready to take up the
A tempo which on a number of occasions follows a brief
ritenuto.

The tone throughout the first section should be bright
and forward. This, together with a marcato rhythm, will
help the impetus which is an essential feature. In the final
bar of the first page, the effect of the crotchet rest followed
by a spacious triplet surges on to a big sound at 'shout'. This
is made the more effective through being on a top E and
preceded by two firmly marcato notes.

The effervescence of this first phrase sets the mood for
much of what is to follow. It should also make the listener
sit up.

Page 3

This calls for a more legato, well sustained and perhaps slightly softer sound. Diction here is important; there are a lot of consonants and the shape of the phrases need thoughtful definition.

Page 4

An exciting crescendo on the top line is here reinforced by the repetition of the words. Bar 6 needs to be really marcato with a crescendo helping the effect. From bars 6 to 10 the ear must work overtime to help tune the accidentals and give full rein to the divisi 2nds and 3rds which are especially effective points of colour. The imitative leads on 'Unto our King . . .' should make their point through a striding tone which takes into account a steady sound on the quavers in 'ser–a–phic-wise'.

Page 5

On the bottom line the singers must listen carefully to the organ. They will then be ready in bars 2 and 3 for *A tempo* in the final bar, with its emphasis on 'Lift'.

Page 6

The first major climax of the anthem comes at 'Glory' where the tone must not only be kept up, but reinforced for the five beats of the first syllable of the word.

Page 7

The faster tempo here should be married to careful diction together with a generously colourful interpretation of $<$ $>$ in bar 3 of the bottom line. *The phrases throughout this middle section are long and therefore need to be expressively moulded.*

Pages 8 and 9

The dynamics here show a general build up of tone through to the first bar of the bottom line of page 9. The steadiness of the groups of quavers on page 9 will be helped by careful articulation of the words. In the last bar of this page the *ritard* in the organ part should be helpful to the singers, provided they are ready for *A tempo* at the top of page 10.

Page 10

The double bar in the bottom line merely signifies the key change. There is no physical gap here, least of all in the words, the complete phrase being 'making ev'ry string More to enravish as they this tune sing'. Therefore no breath should be taken after 'string' or 'enravish'. This latter word—'en –rav – ish' needs colourful treatment, while 'sing' on the top of page 11, although getting softer all the time, must be held for its full seven beats, with an audible final 'g' in evidence.

Page 12

Here, and for much of the next page, the music is a repetition of the first section of the anthem. Being the second time round, it should contain even more interest than before. As the new material which appears on the bottom line of page 13 is only marginally different from page 4, care must be taken to avoid any mistakes.

Page 14

Points mentioned earlier are identical here, not least the need for careful negotiation of the *poco allarg.* in bar 6 together with *A tempo* which follows it.

Page 15

A really big climax must be arrived at here with a full sound on 'the King of <u>Glor</u> – y'. As on previous occasions in this anthem, the crotchet rest in the first bar of the bottom line is an important and subtle point, both of emphasis and colour. The accidentals here in bar 2 must be tuned with accuracy. If anything, the tendency will be to sharpen these intervals.

ORGAN

A mere glance at the organ part immediately shows its importance in the general scheme. As an entirely independent entity it plays a particular role in the architecture and consequently in the overall concept.

The sense of occasion mentioned earlier is set by the authority of the organ introduction in which registration and phrasing play a major part. While repeated notes, as in the first two bars, must have a rhythmic sparkle, rests provide an equally essential factor in setting the scene for what is to follow.

The organ accompaniment contributes a further factor by ensuring that the joins between sections are smoothly and logically negotiated. The first of these, at the bottom of page 2, hinges on choir and organist sensing their togetherness at the beginning of the third bar of the bottom line. This is one of a number of points where joint contact by all concerned is needed.

Page 3

The first note, although by design short, must nevertheless be heard. This will be achieved when the key is depressed down to its bed and then quickly released. The eight semiquavers at the end of the line should be slightly detached but always rhythmically steady.

Pages 4 and 5

If the quavers chatter with some urgency they will help
underline the choir's reiterated insistence on praise.

The bottom line of page 5 contains the second of the
joins. Here, the pedal in bar 3 must, through choice of
suitable stops and rhythmic detachment, leave no possible
doubt in the minds of the singers as to their cue. This is a
difficult moment, made the more so by the low notes on the
pedal.

Page 6

The second bar on the bottom line is a further moment
where the crotchet chords in the right hand, together with
the quavers in the left, must between them determine the
extent of *poco allarg*.

Page 7

An entirely new mood and a new colour emerge in the
second line. Throughout this middle section a flexibly flowing quaver movement must prevail which will forcibly contrast with the two outer sections of the anthem.

Page 9

The final bar is yet another place where choir and organist
must think and move together, but with the organ necessarily dictating the going rate. The same applies in bars 2
and 3 of the bottom line of page 10.

Page 12

From here onwards it is a matter of the same procedure as
in the first section of the anthem.

Page 15

The rests along the bottom line are significant in their relationship to the sustained minims in the voice parts. The final note in the pedal must be given full value if its point—which is an important one—is to be effectively made.

CONDUCTOR

Much of what has already been said applies just as much to the conductor who must take charge in negotiating the changes of speed at the various joins.

At the outset the conductor must clearly indicate the pulse so that there is no doubt as to the length of the initial dotted minim.

Whereas in the outer sections a bold and decisive beat will help all concerned, the middle section needs a much more flowing and relaxed pulse to relay the contrasted style which here predominates.

In the two final bars, the pause, which might well be made into four strict crotchet beats, will be indicated by the right hand, while the left hand will mark the pedal E.

SERIES 3 HOLY COMMUNION
John Rutter
Published by Oxford University Press (S 598)
Recording by RSCM (OLY 131) now deleted

This was the first published setting of the new text. As such, it incorporates some features which were novel at the time, such as the use of short organ introductions to establish the tonality and tempo for the brief responses before and after the Gospel. John Rutter also dispensed with the traditional inflexions for the Sursum Corda, using in their place a single note intonation for the Priest, with a simple reply indicative of the style employed throughout this setting.

The vocal writing throughout is not demanding. Much of it is in unison, a relatively new approach which subsequent composers have adopted though not always with the rhythmic, melodic and harmonic interest which Rutter has cultivated in a particularly personal way, while at the same time being able to write in a basically simple style.

KYRIE

An essentially legato style is called for with each and every minim fully sustained in tone. In bar 3, the stress on the first syllable of '<u>mer</u> – cy' is offset by a lightly shaded final syllable. With the minim coming on the final, and unaccented, syllable on each of the nine occasions when the word 'mercy' is sung, it could so easily be deformed into 'mer – <u>cy</u>'. The expression marks need full colour here, almost to the extent of exaggeration.

GLORIA

The firm one-in-a-bar the composer asks for is a basic must. A determined style, helped by equally firm word clarity in the crotchets, will combine to produce the desired effect. *This is striding music* underlined by a highly charged rhythmic drive. This is seen from the outset where the repeated crotchets must be detached and marcato. As in the Kyrie, so in bar 7 here, a clearly defined accent on the first syllable of 'high–est' will help counteract any tendency to emphasise the second, and unimportant, syllable.

At the end of the second line the mood changes to a more restrained legato. Even so, the crotchets must be light, especially in the recurring ♩♩ rhythm. As the original mood reverts back at the end of the third line, the first page is cast in an ABA form.

Note that page 4 should be no slower than the preceding page. The suspensions in the alto line on 'Christ' and 'Father' should be slightly emphasised as brief moments of harmonic interest.

By thinking of one-in-a-bar, no problems will arise over the juxtaposition of ♩♩ and ♩♩ The same will apply on the duplet in the second bar of *Amen* which will present no problems if sung and played broadly and deliberately.

Although at the end of the top line of page 5 the original mood reappears, the singing throughout is always dictated by long onward moving phrases. To this end, the fewer the breaths the better.

THE GOSPEL

These short phrases move quickly, with the pedal setting the pace in the initial bar. If each response ends in strict time, and with no pause, the impact is the more impressive. In the first response, the repeated crotchets on 'Glory to' should be detached and light.

SURSUM CORDA

The same applies here, except that the music now moves in a $\frac{2}{2}$ pulse. Each response is progressively louder and therefore should sound the more exciting and cumulative. Even in three short and simple responses it is possible to create a sense of occasion.

SANCTUS

As the organ establishes the tempo, this must be carefully and correctly thought out—and in advance. The choir have little option but to follow suit.

A pure 'o' vowel is necessary with the stress coming on the first syllable of '*ho*–ly'. In the second line, the minim should always slightly crescendo through to the third beat. *In this way the phrases will grow musically.*

The overall vocal crescendo from start to finish is a gradual increase in intensity. If it is carefully worked out and progressive, the effect will be the more exciting if *forte* is reached at the last phrase, and not before.

The quavers throughout need to be sung lightly, especially the second of each pair.

ACCLAMATIONS

The organ must give a clear and decisive start, preferably using a reed and moving in *strict* time. In the penultimate bar of each response the pedal should indicate the extent of the broadening asked for.

In the second Acclamation, the first beat of each bar needs a pronounced accent, offset by the second and third crotchets being, by contrast, sung lightly.

The bass of the organ part provides the rhythmic stability throughout.

BENEDICTUS

As in *Sanctus*, the organ sets the pace. Be sure the crotchet at the end of the first three bars is given *full* value. *It is always so easy to hurry up-beats at the end of a bar.*

AGNUS DEI

Without a conductor to indicate the pulse of the initial organ note, the choir *must* look across at each other and decide the tempo. As usual, all quavers must move lightly, especially those coinciding with unaccented words or syllables.

DISMISSAL

This highly effective miniature should be *marcato* and bold, saying the final word in no uncertain way. A slight broadening out, dictated by the bass in bar 2, will add to the overall impressiveness.

ORGAN

From start to finish much depends on the ability of the organist to set the correct tempi and, through registration, the correct mood. The task of the organist is further increased by his almost exclusive responsibility for the harmonic context. Imaginative registration, and contrasted according to the character of the music, will also be helpful. A typical example of this comes in the *Kyrie* where, in the first and third sections, the use of an oboe stop will happily contrast with flutes, and *vice versa*, for the middle section 'Christ, have mercy'.

In the *Gloria*, the crotchet rests are an essential part of the scheme and must be fully observed. By doing so, the strident, authoritative sound will be the more marked, while the use of a Swell Trumpet can add much to the strength of the music. Here, as elsewhere, absolute rhythmic integrity is a necessity while, by an equally marked contrast, bars 13 to 20 and page 4 mirror the voices through being quieter and more legato.

CONDUCTOR

It is seldom likely that a conductor will be available or even,

114 *Making Church Music Work*

in normal circumstances, desirable for music such as this. If, however, there is a conductor, he will assume the role of the organist in deciding the tempi. The main consideration throughout should be as few beats as possible. What was said earlier about the start of the *Agnus Dei* will apply equally to a conductor.

GOD BE IN MY HEAD
John Rutter

Published by Oxford University Press—New York
(Catalogue No. 94. 326)

A first glance at this short piece is deceptively misleading, for it is by no means the easy assignment it would appear to be.

While the prevailing mood certainly demands a controlled legato with a subtle awareness for the phrase shapes, there is much variety within the twenty-five bars of this miniature. This, in its turn, calls for considerable flexibility if the performance is to ring true.

As with so much church music in quadruple time, the crotchets will move the more easily and lightly—which is what the music obviously demands here—if there is a feeling of two-in-a-bar rather than four. In no way must the music become ponderous.

The composer's metronome mark suggests rather more movement than might be expected from this reflective text, the more so if the turgid performances we so frequently hear of Walford Davies' setting of these words are taken as the norm.

Three main considerations need to be constantly borne in mind:

1 *Intervals*. There are recurring danger spots where incorrectly tuned intervals can easily result in unsatisfactory chording. Barely has the anthem begun before there are potential trouble spots as, for example, the bass in bars 2 and 3, where a rising major 6th followed by downward stepwise movement, and then a downward leap of an

octave, combine to provide all the don'ts of text book harmony!

The soprano and bass lines on the top of page 2, together with the tenor in the first bar of the second line, and the bass in the second and third bars of the third line, are all further examples of moves which look easy enough on paper but which must be approached with great care in the matter of accuracy of distance (which is what intervals are all about). *These places can only be negotiated reliably through listening.*

2 *Accidentals.* Having first concentrated on really sharpening the tenor A in bars 7 and 8, the second page is full of accidentals all of which are calculated, as deliberate points of colour, to pull the tonality away from the home key. *All accidentals must first be carefully heard in the mind and then accurately tuned.*

Of special importance are such places as the second line of page 2 where, in the second bar, the tenor A♯ becomes A♮ two beats later. Even more crucial is the bass line which slides down chromatically with a sharpened D at the end of the line—a whole tone up from the previous note (C♯). This particular note is pivotal in bringing the tonality back to E major.

A further instance is the D♮ in bar 3 of the third line. Here the altos and basses must, through listening, help each other to accurately tune their octave which, incidentally, will be hardest for the basses, being a perfect 5th below the previous note.

These are some of the danger points which here, as in countless other instances in unaccompanied choral music, can so easily conspire to upset the pitch.

3 *Phrasing.* Much of the anthem is built in five bar phrases each of which should be sung in one breath so as to maintain both textual continuity and the expressively beautiful contours of the music.

In the initial phrase, tenors and basses should sing lightly especially when, as in bar 2, the movement is not step-wise. (This feature recurs in bar 3 of the second page.) At the outset it is the tenor line which, being the first to move, sets the pace and must therefore be very neatly sung by all concerned.

The crescendo in bar 6 emphasises the slight change of mood which coincides with the key centre moving to B major.

The tenor A♯s, as upward moving parts, must be *fully* sharpened. On the bottom line avoid an ugly vowel sound which could result in two bars of 'lew–king'.

As the altos have two crotchets at the end of page 1, it is best if they take no breath there. This will help the continuity and avoid a snatch breath which could easily produce 'look–*in*'.

On page 2 the same applies at the end of the first bar of the 2nd line. Nor must there be an obvious breath at the end of this line, otherwise the 't' of 'heart' is certain to be untidy and probably too explosive.

The final six bars are more deliberate as the *Poco meno mosso* would suggest. This means a *little* less movement, *not* a lot less. The tenors are given a beautiful little sigh at the end of the third line; this will sound its best if the B is slightly emphasised and the A rounded off.

The pause here will be rhythmic if S.A. and B. minims are made into three crotchet beats with the A in the tenor becoming two beats. The final consonant will then sound on the next crotchet beat with the next bar in strict time. This then becomes a bar of $\frac{6}{4}$:

On the bottom line the singers will have to work hard to make the <><> effective on what are relatively low notes.

In the penultimate bar, the tenors have an eleventh hour fling with a beautifully lyrical four notes which should slightly predominate over the other parts. On the final chord, *ppp* really does mean *very* soft.

Two general points on the words:

1 It is 'God' at the beginning of each phrase, not 'Cod'. The latter results from too much explosion on the initial consonant.

2 The final syllable of each phrase is 'ing', not 'in', which so easily results from lazy speech.

ORGANIST

An initial chord of E major, rather than an octave E, will help the singers to establish the tonality more easily.

CONDUCTOR

The main needs here are to give a beat which will suggest the flow of the music while at the same time allowing for the *rubato* the composer specially asks for. This would seem to apply in two respects:

   a. by leaning on the important words with the less emphatic words correspondingly lightened, and
   b. allowing the shape of the phrases to unfold, especially at the cadence points which need to be rounded off so as to allow the singers time to breathe comfortably.

As always, it is helpful if the conductor sings to himself as he gives the beat.

THE TRUE GLORY

Peter Aston

Published by the RSCM (No. 254)

Recorded at RSCM Golden Jubilee Festival Service (LPB 781)

Peter Aston is one of the few contemporary English composers writing in a simple, but always interesting and thoroughly professional style. Even so, it is hardly surprising that what, on the face of it, appears deceptively easy, demands an unremitting vocal control, careful word clarity and an over-riding sense of long phrases slowly unfolding. Achieve these and even the smallest choir will draw from the music its full impact and sense of occasion.

1st page

The repeated Fs must be cleanly articulated and never with any sense of hurry, the very reverse in fact. This is especially so where there are quavers (bars 4, 6 and 7).

Here and throughout the anthem the $\diamondsuit$ call for a carefully graded control otherwise too swift a crescendo will result.

All four beats of the final note of page 1 must equally relay a calculated diminuendo. Natural word emphasis takes precedence over purely musical considerations. It is not 'There must be a beginning of any great matter' but 'There MUST be a be – GIN – ning of any GREAT matter'.

Page 4

The tenor A ♭ in bar 4 needs careful tuning as will the alto

E♮ at the beginning of the second line. Also, in bar 4, there should be no breath after the word 'end', the first seven bars of this page being one continuous phrase.

As with the final note of the first page, so even more here the final F, tied through to page 5, must be carefully controlled both in length and diminuendo.

Page 5

The F ♯ major tonality established by the organ in bar 4 must immediately be 'felt' by the singers and retained throughout this middle section.

The quavers should move lightly and in a relaxed, flowing way in marked contrast to what went before and will reappear later.

The wide upward intervals (7ths, octaves and 9ths) at the beginning of the second line, together with the similar moves in the third line, require especial care in tuning, the distance involved being further than it might at first seem.

Note that the final syllable of 'accomplished' (bar 32) sounds *on* the first beat of the bar, and as a quick 'sh'd'.

Page 6

In the first and second lines the tuning of the accidentals must be carefully judged and always in relation to each singer *listening* to the overall chording.

In line 2, the final consonant of 'spirit' should be sounded on, and not before, the second beat of the last bar.

In all slow moving music, final consonants need a specially careful and disciplined unanimity. Otherwise, they will be neither neat nor precise.

In bar 4 of the bottom line, the juxtaposition of E flat, F and G within one chord demands accurate tuning and chording. The nature of this unusually beautiful chord needs to be relayed to advantage.

Page 7

The cross-rhythms in bars 3 and 4 dictate a momentary $\frac{2}{4}$ pulse:

1 2	1 2	1 2
a –	ny	great

Page 8

In bar 3, the four semiquavers should be very slightly detached, but never hurried. The dotted quaver at the end of the line must be given full value, almost to the extent of a double dot.

The long diminuendo which commences in the 2nd line is a gradual process which continues through to the final sung note. Cross rhythms again occur at the end of this line and call for similar treatment as previously.

Some emphasis on 'true' will help both the word sense and the triple reiteration of 'the *true* glory'.

ORGAN

Although marked 'pp' at the start, there must be enough support, partly dictated by the size of the choir, for the slender vocal line, while at the same time establishing the harmonic outline. It is in places such as this that an organist must judge how much organ to use, the more so as too much sound will only encourage the choir to sing too loudly.

The right-hand phrasing in the first two bars should be neatly shaped.

Page 4

A soft Swell reed will provide new colour in the second line, while the addition of a Swell trumpet on the final note of this line will further enhance the tonal structure.

Careful timing of the minim chords in the fourth bar of
the bottom line will help the singers with their syncopation,
especially in their hearing the important third beat.

Page 5

The quavers in the second and third lines must be both
distinct and rhythmically clear, echoing as they do a similar
progression in the voice parts. In this way, the organist can
enter into a helpful partnership with those he is accompanying.

Page 6

From the change of key in the second line onwards, the
rhythm and phrase must be clearly defined, much of it
being independent of the voice parts.

Page 8

The semiquavers in bar 4, which re-echo the voice parts in
the previous bar, should be detached in a rhythmically
marked way, though not pecked.

It is best if the penultimate chord of the anthem be
detached only in the right hand. *Niente* means what it
says—nothing—i.e. the softest stop you can find, and, with
the swell box closed.

CONDUCTOR

All that is needed here is for the prevailing mood of the
music to be complemented by a restrained beat which will
primarily indicate the pulse. The left hand can help by
showing the length and cut-off of the long notes at the ends
of phrases. The left hand can also help to mark the word
stresses which, as mentioned earlier, do not necessarily

coincide with what would normally be the rhythmically strong beats.

When the pulse changes from three to four, a clear down beat will help the singers. As with what was suggested for the singers on page 5, so the conductor can further help to project the relaxed mood here, while again indicating with the left hand the length of long notes such as the five beats on 'won' at the bottom of page 5.

After the double bar in the second line of page 6, the conductor can further clarify the rhythm and, on the final page the emphasis on the word 'true' together with the final sung note.

It will thus be seen that a sensitive conductor plays two roles here, that of indicating the basic pulse while, with the left hand, helping to show interpretative points to advantage.

MAKE A JOYFUL NOISE UNTO THE LORD
William Mathias
Published by Oxford University Press A 220
Recorded by Liverpool Cathedral (LPB 663)

A successful and convincing performance of this effervescent and exciting anthem hinges on certain factors:

1 The organist setting, and maintaining with uncompromising accuracy, a highly charged rhythmic scheme.

2 The singers taking up this rhythm in no less exciting a way. The fact that the accompaniment involves only one person and the singing any number, places a degree of corporate responsibility on the singers.

3 The interplay of colour in the accompaniment being contrasted with vocal colour in which the crispness of the words plays an additional role.

4 For all concerned, the process of learning the music should take place at a slow tempo. By doing so, the rhythmic and verbal subtleties will be clearly implanted in the mind, after which it is a matter of gradually speeding up the momentum without any loss of accuracy.

5 Finally, and by no means least, singers and organist must let their hair down and join forces in a thoroughly exciting way, the one complementing the other. The generally accepted notion of church music frequently implies a serious or 'religious' preoccupation which, in music such as this, will do little or no justice to the excitement the composer must have felt in setting what is, after all, a jubilant text.

For the singers, certain rhythms on which the music hinges must first be worked out in isolation and fully assimilated. They must be sung or clapped any number of times until they become second nature. *In all instances the words should help this process.*

Page 1

Bar 6 is a rhythm fundamental to the anthem as an entity. Although the four quavers must necessarily be equal in length, the tendency when singing at the correct speed will be for the fourth quaver to be hurried. This can be counteracted by slightly leaning on the third quaver as the second main beat of the bar. This, and the crotchet on the third beat, to which the quaver is tied, must be given *full* value. Accuracy will be made the easier if the choir are aware of, and listen to, the minim chord in the organ part. If the four quavers are in any way hurried, the rhythm can easily become distorted into something resembling

to the   Lord

Page 2

A variant of this distinctive rhythm is seen in bars 2 and 4 where, as later on pages 4 and 5, the same principle applies, although in the latter instance the particular underlay of the words helps. In bars 7 to 9, and in the following three bars, the syncopation must never be hurried. The main beats must be firmly felt while, through careful verbal articulation, there will be a steadying influence. It must be remembered that the final note in bar 7, and again in bar 10, is only a quaver, whereas in bars 8 and 11 the final quaver is a rest. This is a quick and subtle move, the more so when sung at the correct speed. It will, moreover, only be heard as a rest when the preceding word, 'is', is *very* short. Great concentration of mind is needed every time these rhythms or their variants appear. The excitement of the music can so easily be adversely reflected through a fatal tendency to hurry.

Having established these important rhythms, the voice parts must now be looked at in more detail:

Page 1

'*joy*–ful' must be emphatic, both for rhythmic purposes and because of what the anthem is all about.

'lands' is four full crotchet beats, with the final consonant sounding quickly and neatly on the fifth beat.

Page 2

In bars 2 and 4 the final 'ss' must be a quick and short sound *on* the fourth beat.

The eight quavers in bar 5, each having a separate word or syllable allocated to them, are relatively easy to negotiate. Less easy is the subsequent tie over the bar, in which the crotchet must be given its full value.

The rhythm in bars 7 and 10, which were discussed earlier, will be helped on its way through neat and crisp diction.

Note that there is no organ here to act as a steadying influence.

Page 3

Here the mood changes and becomes rather more legato through the more pronounced crotchet movement. The rests are an important feature of the rhythmic scheme here, while the alto part in bars 5 and 9 help to provide some interesting points of colour through the seconds which clash with the treble on the main beats. In terms of dynamics, the carefully graded 'poco a poco dim' throughout the course of this page is important.

It is so easy for an anthem such as this to be loud for most of the time. The bare fifths in the last two bars and over the page are a further point of colour, the emphasis of which is heightened by a reasonably detached style of singing. In the final bar of the page it is '*peo*–ple'.

Page 4

The consecutive fourths which are such a characteristic trade mark of the composer provide further additional colour here. The music progressively becomes busier and busier and will continue to do so with increasing momentum through to the end. This, together with the dynamic increase from *mp* to *ff* is a further reason for a discipline which will combat any temptation for the pulse to quicken.

Page 5

The imitative points in lines 2 and 3 add further excitement, although the crotchets and minims should in themselves provide a steadying influence on the rhythm. A firm tone and sense of authority must prevail here.

Pages 4 and 5 will be the more rhythmically assured if all voices are constantly listening to each other.

Page 6

Ideally, no breath should be taken along the top line. Taking breath will only result in a clipped sound on 'endu – reth'.

The Amens should be sung as marked, in strict time with the final syllable of the first two deliberately short and staccato. This is for a special effect.

The final Amen must be carefully counted—and in strict time. The organ is the main means of ensuring that all end together and at the split-second moment. The cut-off here is a further special effect and must be electrifying. The end

of the anthem then becomes most exciting, the organ having the final word, and with all the stops out.

This is an example of music where the rhythmic vitality
and cumulative intensity will be further heightened
through a similar vitality in the diction and general word
clarity.

When performing music such as this, singers do not
alway realise the extent to which they must spit out and
exaggerate the words and the detached quavers. It will
demand hard work and a style alien to many an English
singer, for whom a sustained legato is usually a more palat-
able proposition.

ORGAN

The entirely independent accompaniment throughout is an
integral part of the scheme. In itself it is as much reliant on
the voices as the voices are on the organ. The one fits like a
glove into the other.

Page 1

The first four bars set the pace, style and mood. The prevailing staccato calls for the use of mutations and therefore
plenty of sparkle. It is a bright, brittle and almost metallic
sound in which the rests are an integral part of the scheme.
They must therefore be given full value, especially the
quaver rests, to allow the impact of the music to be fully
realised.

The importance of rhythmic accuracy in bar 3 was mentioned earlier in relation to the voice parts, while the correct placing of the minim chord in bar 6 will help the singers
to be aware of the third beat of the bar.

Page 2

As the organ part in the first five bars is identical to that of the singers, it can help reinforce the rhythmic security of the voices. It will also help to lessen some of the problems mentioned earlier.

In bars 6 and 9 and at similar places throughout page 3, the short quaver figures act as rhythmic continuity, dove-tailing the ends of the vocal phrases. When, as repeatedly happens here, the organ comes in after a bar rest, it must be with rhythmic accuracy. It is therefore necessary to count more during the rests than when actually playing.

Pages 4 and 5

The organ continues to stabilise the rhythmic pulse through the continuous succession of staccato quavers.

Page 6

There must be absolute accuracy in lines 2 and 3. This merely reiterates what was said earlier in connection with rhythm and rests. In the final four bars more than anywhere previously, the singers must count and listen to the organist who takes the ultimate responsibility here as in so much of this anthem.

Registration must be carefully worked out in advance and should be marked in the copy. This will ensure that the various grades of dynamics are relayed to advantage while providing the necessarily independent range of colour.

CONDUCTOR

There is more justification for a conductor here than in any of the other examples we have so far discussed.

The task is a fundamentally simple one, that of indicating a strict four-in-a-bar from start to finish. A smallish but uncompromisingly rhythmic beat is all that is needed, with slightly more emphasis on the first beat of each bar. This acts as a stabilising influence.

These are the aids by which a conductor who is in confident control can help to co-ordinate the individual roles of the choir and the organist.

The left hand should be used to indicate entries and as a check for the duration of the long notes on the final pages.

Giocoso e ritmico implies a vitality and a sense of joy. It must never be taken to mean anything approaching a break-neck speed. As has been said a number of times in connection with this anthem, rhythm is the basis of its credibility.

FERIAL RESPONSES

The simplest and most practical all-purpose version is that published by the Royal School of Church Music.

Although printed in the key of G, these often sound better if transposed up a semitone into A♭, especially if they are sung unaccompanied. For an efficient choir the key of A is not out of the question, nor is this too high for the average congregation.

A little imagination can make these miniatures into something of a memorable experience. They will stand the test of weekly repetition if all concerned in their performance, and that includes the priest, set out to give them something of a new look and thus avoid any semblance of the dullness which routine can so easily produce.

Four general pointers should underline the singing of each example:

1 Speech rhythm, in other words their moving at the normal pace of deliberate speech but with the natural inflexions, emphasis, and lightness on unimportant words and syllables which should always be basic points of departure in any singing. A television newscaster is a good model.

2 The importance of accurate chording, especially major and minor 3rds.

3 The need to give some thought as to how expression marks can add to the overall interest. If the responses are to be accompanied, this also applies to the organist. It is so unimaginative to hear each response sung at virtually the same dynamic level and speed, except possibly the

sentimental habit of the final response being soft and slow.

4 Although written out mainly in semibreves and minims—which is merely for convenience—flexibility and movement will be helped the more if crotchets and quavers are thought of as the norm.

THE OPENING SET

1st response

The accents here are '. . . *shew* forth thy *praise*'

Despite the melodic rise, the important word to be emphasised is the verb 'shew' not 'forth' as so often happens when singing this response.

A robust tone with firm articulation is indicated here with care for the clarity of syllables in 'forth thy' where the two 'th's should not be run into each other and become 'forthy'.

2nd response

Some contrast is needed here with a gentler dynamic as a basis. The words 'haste to' will need care to avoid the two 't's becoming 'hays–to'.

3rd response

The commas in the priest's part of the Gloria need to be only slightly marked. This will avoid three disjointed statements and it can then be sung in one breath. In the choir response a slight crescendo will increase the momentum of the reciting notes. As with the priest's part, so here it is best if the comma after 'beginning' is only marginal.

Careful stressing of the important words will also help, e.g.
'and <u>ev</u>er <u>shall</u> be, <u>world</u> without <u>end</u>. <u>A</u>men'.

The basses need to stride firmly so as to add authority
both to the words and the harmonic outline. 'Withou–<u>tend</u>'
will be avoided by softening the final 't' of 'without'.

4th response

This is the most emphatic response so far. It needs to be
reasonably brisk, vital and loud, if a convincing sense of
climax is to be projected.

In terms of practicalities, it is at this point that the ener-
gies of many choir members are focused not on what they
are singing but on finding the psalm which is to follow.

THE CREED, LESSER LITANY AND LORD'S PRAYER

On all counts it is probably best in most circumstances for
this section to be said, although choir and congregation
must reply in as firm and convincing a way as should the
priest declaim his part. Whether said or sung, phrasing is a
must:

'<u>Lord</u>, have <u>mer</u>cy upon us' etc.

For the Creed and Lord's Prayer it is always more satisfactory and logical for the people not to repeat the priest's
introduction 'I believe in God' and 'Our Father'.

If only we would bring to both a new look and a new
experience every time we say them. This is so easy if we
take care to think about and relay their inner meaning. It is
especially relevant in such statements as 'Thy <u>kingdom</u>
come, Thy <u>will</u> be done' where we invariably, and incorrectly, accent the verb.

THE SECOND SET

1st response

The natural word stresses should mirror the musical pattern:

    'And grant us thy sal – <u>VA</u> – tion'

This avoids the indefensible 'sal–va–SHERN'

2nd response
Similarly here:

    'And <u>mer</u> – cifully <u>hear</u> us when we <u>call</u> up – on <u>thee</u>'

3rd response

the priest must avoid falling into the all too easy trap of singing 'rye–cheous–ness'. Phonetically, it is '<u>ry</u>–tee–ous–ness'.

   The response should be loud, dynamic and convincing, with the emphasis on the crux of the statement, '<u>JOY</u>–ful' thus avoiding 'joy–FULL' which is almost certain to be further exaggerated by the melodic drop of a third.

4th response

A gentler sound here will contrast well with the preceding response.

   The priest should endeavour to shade off the word '<u>peo</u>–ple', with the choir similarly treating 'in–<u>heri</u>–tance'.

5th response

Here the response needs a colourful and rather more urgent treatment with an accompanying crescendo through to the end where the alto D♯ needs to be clearly marked as the third of the first major chord to be encountered for some time—'but only <u>thou</u>, O God'.

6th response

The words here suggest the reverse of the quiet treatment to which the text is so frequently subjected. It is surely something of an emphatic plea; whatever else may happen, do not take the Holy Spirit from us. With this in mind, the response should be only fractionally slower and quieter than its predecessor.

AMENS

These produce the best sound when subjected to a firm and reasonably brisk treatment. The major 3rd (i.e. the alto in the first chord and the tenor in the second) carry the same responsibility as anywhere else while the striding bass adds to the emphasis. Each Amen can, and should, be treated differently with, for example, the third collect at Evensong being quieter and slightly slower.

ORGAN

If these are to be accompanied, a light support is all that is needed. The pedal can be used in the more emphatic and therefore louder responses, while the reflective examples are preferable on manuals only. Stop changes can be a further help in respect of relaying the mood of the words. As with psalm accompaniment, some playing 'over the top' will add further variety, especially when the singers are self-dependent:

And take not thy Holy Spirit from us

is but one of many possibilities in this respect.

CONDUCTOR

All that is needed is a clear, but small, first and last beat to each response, with the left hand helping to emphasise important words and syllables.

PSALMS

Although the Cathedral Psalter with its unendearing emphasis on heavy type suggests something far removed from the speech rhythm of our more enlightened times, the underlying principle of singing the psalms should always be that the music fits the *natural* inflexions, and the rise and fall of normal deliberate speech. This principle applies to all types of psalm singing, though it is obviously less easy to apply this to the blackest of Cathedral Psalters than to the very latest in speech rhythm.

What follows holds good for virtually any type of pointing, providing the application of the principles is approached in a logically consistent way.

A guideline which should constantly be borne in mind is that whereas in the Cathedral Psalter type of pointing the words were made to be subservient to the musical claims of the chant, the reverse obtains in speech rhythm where the music is secondary, and rightly so, to the pointing itself.

While reiterating that the words, and with them the pointing, are the prime consideration, the personality of each and every psalm, complete with its underlying mood and character, must determine the speed and dynamic range of performance. Whereas Psalm 137, if it is to be plaintive, measured and deliberate—and this would seem an obvious way to project the full impact of the desolation of the captives in Babylon—then Psalm 150, as a triumphant paean of praise, will move with a greater feeling of vitality, excitement, and even urgency.

A change of mood is often encountered within a psalm, most frequently, as in Psalm 6, when a penitential section suddenly gives way to a mood of profound hope and joy.

This, that, and more may happen to the sinful man, 'but as for me, I will rejoice and praise God'. A similar mood prevails in Psalm 37 where, after thirty-nine extremely beautiful and thoughtful verses, the psalmist suddenly produces the sting in the tail to which he was often prone.

These verbal contrasts must be reflected—and carried one stage further in their meaningfulness—through not only a change of mood but, in musical terms, through pace and music. This should even extend to the type of tone a choir will produce. Just as a sad, despondent, or weary tone of speech will sound very different from that of joy, celebration and gratitude, so must the music match and colour these changes.

In every instance it is the impact of the words which is the governing factor.

Having established that the psalms are full of a multitude of moods, wonderful in their range and dramatic impact, it is quite indefensible to sing every psalm at virtually the same speed and with the minimum of dynamic variation. This is an unimaginative as the treatment regularly meted out *ad nauseam* to many a hymn. Yet this is precisely what does happen Sunday by Sunday in many a church.

The poetry of the psalter is a unique experience and the musician must do all in his power to grasp this beauty, to assimilate it, to live with and, most essential of all, to relay the fullness of its message across to the worshipper. Then, and only then, will the psalms become an aid to worship instead of a distraction.

Psalm 15

As a point of departure this psalm, as it appears in *The Parish Psalter*, is probably as good an example as any. Apart from the final verse, it plays no awkward tricks and is consequently a useful model.

The pace should be a moderate one determined by the prevailing mood of the text. Verse 1 asks a simple question which is answered, and qualified, in some detail in verses 2 to 6. Verse 7 sums it all up with the same brevity as was the question posed in the first verse.

Assuming the choirmaster insists on an intelligent approach to psalm singing, and persists until he gets it, a choir will quickly learn by instinct and example how to phrase. The ruling factor must always be the emphasising of key words and syllables together with the consequent lightening of unimportant words. Commas, as means of punctuation, must be neither prolonged nor rushed.

Verse 1 serves as a model for all the verses. By leaning on 'Lord', 'dwell', 'rest' and 'ho–ly hill', and by similarly lightening the remainder of the text, everything will fall into place and produce that natural style of phrasing which we conveniently term speech rhythm.

Verse 2. A subtle point here is 'uncor–rupt life' where the natural stress should be 'uncor' and not 'uncor'. It is far too easy to fall into the trap of almost automatically stressing the first note of each verse and half verse.

In verse 2 it should be 'Even he', while the second quarter begins 'and doeth', whereas the word 'He' which is common to the start of verses 3 to 6 is an important word in the context of the psalm as an entity.

Verse 3. 'nor done evil to his neighbour' while, after the colon, the words move quickly 'and hath not slandered'. This is the very opposite of the Cathedral Psalter thump in, for example, *Nunc Dimittis*: 'ER – cording to thy word'.

Verse 4. The two notes on 'own' must be sung lightly and nimbly so as to avoid what otherwise could be 'oh–own'. The same applies in the second half of verse 5. 'fear' should be unhurried if it is to give its full impact.

Verse 6. 'money. upon usury' must be unhurried so that the vowels and syllables have time to be clearly heard. Note that 'money' and 'upon' are each allocated a separate note. It is *not* 'money up.on'.

Verse 7. The singing here should mirror exactly how this phrase would be spoken, but obviously omitting the colon.

GLORIA It is all too easy for slackness to creep in here. A combination of familiarity, relaxation after concentration on the psalm, even to the extent of finding the next piece of music at the same time, can all combine to make the Gloria sound like a damp squib instead of the final utterance which 'Christianises' what has gone before. Our subscribing in convincingly enthusiastic terms, glory to the Trinity from the beginning of time, now and through to eternity, should become a crescendo of tone and intensity, both in the words and in the music. The sum total of sound should induce a sense of excitement which ideally should increase the more we sing the Gloria.

MUSIC The chant by Arnold, as found in *The Parish Psalter*, is as harmless as are most single chants. It therefore needs imaginative treatment with the sopranos striving their hardest to produce a musically shaped phrase, the basses a firm and neatly poised line, while the altos and tenors lightly fill in the notes which complete the harmonic structure.

There are various possible musical permutations. The first and last verses could, for example, be sung in unison, with the last verse a firm and authoritative utterance summing up, as suggested earlier, all that has gone before.

Verse 5 could be tenors and basses in unison, with verse 6 similarly treated by the sopranos. Alternatively, the psalm could be sung in harmony throughout.

These are only suggestions but they show something of the variety of treatment which is possible, the more so when the dynamic range is carefully varied. Moreover, if these permutations are regularly changed at each performance it will help to keep the choir on its toes.

CONDUCTOR What was said on page 136 concerning the conducting of responses applies equally here. The need for economy of gesture so that points of emphasis can be given their full effect, is an essential factor which should always be uppermost in the conductor's mind.

HYMNS

The singing and playing of hymns repeatedly proves to be a stumbling block. Choirs who prepare anthems and settings with great care and perform them with real artistry are frequently guilty of a slipshod attitude towards hymns paralleled by the attitude of many an organist towards the playing of them. A certain something seems to surround hymns, a familiarity which, if it does not exactly breed contempt, certainly breeds carelessness, the more so when this is allied to a conviction that hymns are easy.

Equally regrettable is the attitude of mind which seems to instinctively relegate hymns to a category akin to second class citizenship. Some choirmasters will even encourage their choirs to view hymns as a necessary evil or an unwarranted intrusion to be dispensed with as quickly as possible in favour of more meaty fare. This not surprisingly leads to their being unrehearsed, uncared for, unimaginative, and in performance thoroughly uninspiring.

By contrast, hymns sung and played well can have a tremendous impact on a service and on those taking part, whether in choir or congregation.

A further contributory factor is the number of brilliant performers who seem utterly incapable of playing hymns with any conviction. These are often the very people whose playing of anthems and voluntaries induces a memorable experience for all concerned, yet when it comes to hymns reveals a blank spot.

If hymns are thought of as dull, they will certainly sound dull. Vitality is as much an essential to hymnody as to any other aspect of church music.

142   *Making Church Music Work*

It must always be remembered that in any church service hymns will be the one certain musical addition. They are a basic and inescapable point of musical departure.

The two examples which follow, the one robust and the other more reflective, must, for our purposes here, suffice. What is suggested in terms of their treatment can be applied and adapted to any hymn. The basic principles are always identical.

FIRMLY I BELIEVE AND TRULY
Tune: *Halton Holgate*
Ancient and Modern Revised (1950 Edition) No. 186

Words

This is great poetry. While Elgar captured their spirit and greatly enhanced them in *The Dream of Gerontius*, the tune by Boyce, although employing simpler and more direct means, nevertheless projects the strength of these words in no less convincing a way (even if the music in this instance was written nearly 200 years before the words).

From the outset, the text is concerned with relaying Christian convictions in no uncertain terms. The very first word sets the pace which is kept up throughout leading on to the final verse, a doxology of unusual construction centring not so much on glory as on adoration.

The tune, which we shall consider later, is in its strength an admirable partner to the words. It is beautifully constructed and in such a way that each and every point of importance in the text is enhanced through the music. Essential nouns, such as those which in the first and last verses affirmatively declaim the Trinity, are no less relevant than 'thought and deed' (verse 2), also 'Light and life' and 'Him the Holy, him the Strong' in verse 3.

Certain verbs and adverbs vie for equal emphasis. The very first line of the hymn, 'trust and hope' (verse 2), 'And I love supremely, solely' (verse 3) are cases in point.

Music

The melodic line, which is of much strength, is beautifully and purposefully constructed. There is always an inevitable feeling of shape which carries the contours on through to the points of climax, such as the high notes at the end of the third line.

The supporting harmonies, while straightforward, have an equal strength and are helped by the striding bass line. In music such as this, it is necessary to give the crotchet passing notes plenty of time so as to allow the harmonies to unfold spaciously. Care should be taken to ensure that the final chord is given its *full* two beats.

Music and words together

The combination of words and music means that the one enriches and strengthens the other. In terms of injecting this or any other hymn with the maximum of colour, variety and interpretation, there are many possible openings. One suggested scheme, dictated by the words, could be:

Verse 1   Unison and fairly loud, the mood underlined by a determined robustness.

Verse 2   Harmony. mf. A more relaxed mood here which by contrast will therefore be more sustained.

Verse 3   The first two lines sopranos only. A crescendo in the second line will help the cumulative effect of 'light', 'life' and 'strength'. The third and fourth lines could be louder and sung by the tenors and basses in unison, with a crescendo throughout leading to the climax on the final word ('Strong').

Verse 4   As verse 2 but perhaps unaccompanied.

Verse 5   All voices in unison, with a broadening out of tempo in the final line. Punctuation here should be carefully articulated but not overdone.

It must be emphasised that this is only a suggested method of approach. In some churches it would be both impossible and undesirable to sing unaccompanied, while the division of voices with certain lines sung by sopranos and others by the men would clearly be impracticable in a church where a large congregation expects to sing every word of every hymn. Some flexibility is therefore necessary. Nor would one suggest that any arrangement of voices which may be worked out would be slavishly followed every time the hymn is sung.

JESU, THE VERY THOUGHT OF THEE

Tune: *Metzler's Redhead*

Ancient and Modern Revised (1950 Edition) No. 189

This has been chosen, and there are frequent examples in this category, as one where the tune is normally associated with other words. *Metzler's Redhead* usually partners the Ascensiontide hymn *Jesu, our hope, our heart's desire* (AMR 146).

What is therefore generally interpreted as a robust tune married up to robust words needs to assume a gentler character when associated with *Jesu, the very thought of thee*. This, moreover, is a two way process which necessitates a similarly gentle approach to the words.

Words

Much of what was said about *Firmly I believe and truly* applies not only here but to any hymn. Basic principles in terms of phrase, punctuation and clarity of diction contribute as much here as anywhere else towards a credibility of performance.

To sing all ten verses would be something of a marathon, a waste of energy, and a certain method of achieving little less than boredom. As the hymn falls naturally, and probably by design, into two distinct parts, it is best to think of it as two separate entities.

Verse 1   An audible comma after the first word is unnecessarily fussy. A slight stress on the word 'Jesu' is all that is needed. Although the music begins on an up-beat, the correct stressing of 'Je–su' demands a strong accent. In line 2, 'sweet–ness' must be neatly articulated; 'breast' is another of those awkward words discussed elsewhere and in which the final 'st' can prove difficult. Lines 1 and 2 should be sung as one continuous phrase.

Verse 2   In line 3 it is 'Jesu's name' not 'Jesus name'

Verse 3   'hope', 'joy', 'kind' and 'good' all need some emphasis as words underlining the essence of the verse.

Verse 4   In the first line a distinct and clearly marked comma should occur after 'find'. While choir and organist must clearly indicate this, it does not extend to the comma after 'Ah' which merely needs to be sung as a sigh. A convincing join at the end of the first and third lines is a must if the words are to express any coherence.

Verse 5   As in verse 3 so here certain words call for special emphasis—'joy', 'prize', 'glory' and 'e – <u>ter</u> – nity'.

In Part 2 the process continues in much the same way, except that what was a gentle image in Part 1 gives place to a more robust style. The words here are positive, strong, and in no way reflective. This mood should be paralleled in the music through a more determined tempo, dynamic and general approach.

Music

The melodic outline is a sturdy one. Although there are only five intervals in movement which is otherwise entirely by step, these intervals are an important part of the scheme. The upward octave near the beginning must be as neatly and accurately tuned as the smaller intervals in the third and fourth lines, probably more so. The bass provides the stamina one would expect and must always be sung with a rhythmic alertness which dictates a slightly detached style.

As in so many hymn tunes, the relatively uneventful tenor and the even less memorable alto line must somehow be made to sound interesting, even if they are poor relations. In general terms, the music has drive which is further increased by the brightness of the key.

Bearing in mind what was said about the contrasted character of each part of this hymn, the style of performance should reflect the text and the variety of sentiments being expressed.

STARTING FROM SCRATCH
How to set about learning new music

Some general guidelines

1 *Selecting music within the resources at your disposal*
   This should never be dictated solely by any preference or personal wish however well intentioned. The ability of a choir must always be the determining factor and the consequent point of departure. Every choir should be presented with a challenge to work at and bite on, but not to be overwhelmed by what they know to be beyond their reasonable capabilities and which therefore acts as a depressive rather than a stimulus.

2 *Presenting the music to the choir*
   We all know that first impressions are often the deepest and the most lasting.
   It is all a question of salesmanship, or how you present your goods. If you, as choirmaster, are uncertain or lukewarm, your choir will be less than receptive. If you are enthusiastic, having done your homework and prepared the music in such a way that you really know all there is to be know about it, you will have little difficulty in convincing your singers or of selling it to them. You must make it your business to persuade the choir, individually or as a whole, that the music in question is neither too hard nor too easy. You, and you alone, must sell your credibility and that of your music.
   At the outset you should say something, as briefly as possible, about the words, the music and the general style of the piece. In terms of the time needed to learn it, some indication should be given as to the intended date

of performance. A choir has little idea of the going rate
or sense of immediacy when told 'We'll perform it when
we know it'. Any self-respecting church choir needs a
dateline as much as does a choral society. The agreed
date must be adhered to (if it is one of the Church's festi-
vals there is no option), but this decision must be a
realistic one never providing too short or unduly long a
time for adequate preparation.

If music can be learned reasonably quickly, the interest
and enthusiasm of the choir is the more likely to be
retained. A dateline soon dispels any image of having all
the time in the world and replaces it with a realistic sense
of reasonable urgency. All of this is dependent on having
a plan of rehearsal action so that the choir and the
choirmaster are able to see the music taking shape, and
with it a growing confidence among the singers.

3 *How to learn the music*
(a) First sing it through, having drawn the attention of
the singers to the key, time and any awkward moments
which are likely to be encountered. In S. S. Wesley's
Blessed be the God and Father the joins between the
recits. and the ensuing sections are examples of this. It
will be necessary to explain how to navigate these.
(b) Ensure that the singers understand how to deal with
any tricky rhythms as in William Mathias' *Make a joyful
noise*. Notes which may present difficulties, awkward
intervals and accidentals all come into this category. (See
John Rutter's *God be in my head*.)
(c) If the music is unaccompanied, help the choir a little
in the initial stages by using the organ or preferably the
piano. This will depend on the ability of the choir. There
will be times when they should be thrown in at the deep
end, others when they need some guidance to stimulate
confidence. The security engendered by holding a child's
hand in the initial stages of learning how to walk is a
parallel here.

(d) Similarly, if the music is accompanied, help the singers a little by quietly playing any really difficult leads. This will usually quicken up the process of learning.

In all these instances be prepared to guide your singers.

(e) Mistakes matter less at this initial stage than the need to sing with confidence and an awareness for the feel of the music.

The early stages of learning the notes is the time to make mistakes.

A tentative attitude, guardedly following your neighbour and leaving out any difficult notes or intervals, will only prolong the process of actual learning. *If you are going to make mistakes make them confidently—and NOW.*

(f) The process of singing through a piece needs to be repeated two or three times. On each occasion certain mistakes will right themselves, others will need some explanation and correction. Once a choir is shown how to remedy mistakes it will gain in confidence and be aware of progress. This, through acquaintance, will start to complete the process which in the end will spell out full accuracy and security.

(g) The next stage is that of working in detail, phrase by phrase. By isolating awkward spots and going back over them a number of times, the process of building will be continued to advantage. Convenient phrase shapes in music such as in Peter Aston's *The true glory* make for an admirable model in this respect. Walmisley in D minor is another apt example with its contrasted SSA and TB phrases making for interesting variety. Not all music will fall so easily into a convenient rehearsal pattern, nevertheless some fundamental approach will need to be worked out on similar lines.

(h) A choir should by now begin to see some return for its efforts. This is the time to shift concentration away from the notes, which by this stage should anyhow be able to more or less look after themselves, on to such

matters as accuracy of chording, balance between the
parts and awareness for expressions marks. Rhythmic
subtleties, such as in William Mathias' *Make a joyful
noise*,which here form a fundamental part of the overall
scheme, must be concentrated on.

(j)   Style is a further consideration. Is the piece basically
in a detached style or is it essentially smooth and
sustained? Is it perhaps a combination of both, such
as in the Gloria of John Rutter's Series 3 Communion Service where the ABA form employs a sustained middle section flanked on either side by a
more brittle and highly charged rhythmic content.

These then are some of the ways through which a new
work might be dealt with. The process is much the same as
that of building a house. After the foundations have been
securely laid we add bricks, plaster, and finally the paint-
work which provides the colour—and the finishing touch.

This sequence of events has its parallel no less in music
than in any other art form.

All this presupposes one fundamental necessity, that of
the choirmaster and / or the organist having done their
homework well in advance. Any instability, be it through
wrong notes, rhythmic faltering or uncertainty in any other
respect as to the know-how of teaching a choir, will be
quickly sensed by the singers for whom it will be inhibiting.

8

Check list of anthems

compiled by DAVID PATRICK

PLEASE NOTE

1 No verse anthems as such have been included.

2 The choice has been on an SATB basis, though occasional simple divisi are included.

3 As one of the objects of this list is to provide suggestions for new material, certain examples have been purposely omitted. Parry's *I was glad*, Purcell's *Rejoice in the Lord*, and S. S. Wesley's *Blessed be the God and Father* come into this category through their familiarity and their frequent use in many churches.

4 The small choice of Christmas music is deliberate, since there is so much to choose from, the bulk of it being readily accessible in collections such as *Carols for Choirs* (OUP).

5 Organ accompaniments to Tudor anthems are specified where revised editions have been issued in line with present day thinking on this matter.

6 It will be noticed that a considerable amount of what is included in the lists is marked as being out of print. The

widespread deletions from publishers' catalogues are a source of concern to all connected with church music. It must however be remembered that publishers will frequently give permission for their own out of print music to be reproduced. *In all instances permission must first be sought*.

David Patrick is also preparing similar recommended lists of anthems for ATB and SSA or unison. These will be available from the RSCM.

List of abbreviations

* Unaccompanied
ø Out of print

16cAB	16th Century Anthem Book (OUP)
AECM	An Anthology of English Church Music (Chester)
AFC	Anthems for Choirs (OUP)
Arr.	Arranged
B & F	Bayley & Ferguson
B & H	Boosey & Hawkes
CAB	The Church Anthem Book (OUP)
CB	Choir Book (RSCM)
CC	Church Choir Library (Stainer & Bell)
CE	Carols for Easter (RSCM)
CFC	Carols for Choirs (OUP)
CMS	Church Music Society (OUP)
COC	Cross of Christ (RSCM)
CSB	Choral Service Book (RSCM)
CUP	Cambridge University Press
E	English
EA	12 Easy Anthems (RSCM)
EAB	The Oxford Easy Anthem Book (OUP)
ED	Exultate Deo (Chappell)
EECM	Early English Church Music (Stainer & Bell)
F	French
FP	Faith Press
FSB	Festival Service Book (RSCM)
G	German
GL	The Giver of Life (RSCM)
GSL	God so loved the world (RSCM)

HFM	Harvest Festival Music (RSCM)
KOG	King of Glory (Novello)
L	Latin
LD	Laudate Dominum (Chappell)
MFS	Motets of the Flemish School (Chester)
MHC	Music for Holy Communion (Motets) (RSCM)
MT	Musical Times (Novello)
NAB	Novello Anthem Book (Novello)
OBC	Oxford Book of Carols (OUP)
ORG	Organ
OUP	Oxford University Press
RSCM	Royal School of Church Music
SB	Service Book (RSCM)
S & B	Stainer & Bell
SEA	Short & Easy Anthems (Novello)
SNCB	Sydney Nicholson Commemoration Book (RSCM)
STS4	Something to Sing (Vol. 4) (CUP)
TCM	Tudor Church Music (OUP)
TECM	Treasury of English Church Music (Blandford)
TFB	Triennial Festival Book (RSCM)
UMP	United Music Publishers
YBP	Year Book Press (Chappell)
YS	York Series (Banks)

Collections of Anthems & Motets

anthems for All Seasons (Chappell)
Anthems for Choirs (Vols. 1 & 4) (OUP)
5 Anthems for Today (RSCM)
An Anthology of English Church Music (Chester)
Christmas and Advent Motets for 4 voices (Chester)
The Church Anthem Book (OUP)
Early English Church Music (Stainer & Bell)
12 Easy Anthems (RSCM)
Exultate Deo (Motets of the Renaissance) (Chappell)
King of Glory (Novello)
Laudate Dominum (Motets of the Renaissance) (Chappell)
Motets of the English School for 4 voices (Chester)
Motets of the Flemish School for 4 voices (Chester)
Motets of the German School for 4 voices (Chester)
Motets of the Italian School for 4 voices (Chester)
Motets of the Spanish School for 4 voices (Chester)
Music for Holy Communion (22 Motets) (RSCM)
Musica Britannica (Stainer & Bell) (Selected volumes only)
The Novello Anthem Book (Novello)
The Oxford Easy Anthem Book (OUP)
Palestrina – 10 four part Motets (OUP)
Short and Easy Anthems (Sets 1 & 2) (Novello)
Sing to the Lord (Novello)
A Sixteenth Century Anthem Book (OUP)
Treasury of English Church Music (Blandford)

Composer & Title	Resources	Publisher	Publisher's Reference	Collection in which included (if applic.)	Comments
ADVENT					
ANON (16th Century)					
"Rejoice In The Lord Alway"	SATB*	OUP φ Peters Novello	TCM 55 H 1528 29013007	φ CB 2 16c AB	Formerly attributed to John Redford (Advent IV)
THOMAS ATTWOOD (1767–1838)					
"Enter Not Into Judgement"	SATB & ORG	Banks φ Novello	YS 247 MT 217		
"Teach Me O Lord"	SATB & ORG	Novello Banks RSCM	29022507 YS 246 SB 6	AFC I	(Advent II) Also suitable for Sexagesima
J. S. BACH (1685–1750)					
"Zion Hears Her Watchmen's Voices"	SATB & ORG	φ Novello	Anthem 1255	φ TFB 1954 NAB	From Cantata "Sleepers Wake"
ADRIAN BATTEN (c. 1580–c.1637)					
"Lord We Beseech Thee"	SATB & ORG (ad lib)	OUP	'TCM 76	16c AB	Also suitable for Lent. Coupled with "When The Lord Turned Again"

Composer / Title	Voicing	Publisher	Catalogue No.		Notes
BENJAMIN BRITTEN (1913—1976) "A Hymn of St Columba"	SATB & ORG	B & H	CCS 67	—	Also suitable for general use L & E
MAURICE GREENE (1695—1755) "Lord Let Me Know Mine End"	SATB & ORG	OUP	—	—	Also suitable for Lent. Contains Soprano Duet
JACOB HANDL (1550—1591) "Obsecro Domine"	SATB*	Müller/Novello	82150104	—	L. only
GEOFFREY HANSON (1939—) "People Look East"	SATB*	Roberton	85037	—	
ZOLTÁN KODÁLY (Arr) (1882—1967) "Veni, Veni, Emmanuel"	SAB*	B & H	CCS 70	—	
HENRY G. LEY (1887—1962) "Come Thou Long Expected Jesus"	SATB & ORG	OUP	E 24	FSB 6 EAB	Bass part divides towards the end
FELIX MENDELSSOHN (1809—1847) "Sleepers Wake, A Voice Is Calling"	SATB & ORG	Banks ∅Novello	YS 441 MT 70	AFC I	Also suitable for St John the Baptist

ADVENT (Continued)

Composer & Title	Resources	Publisher	Publisher's Reference	Collection in which included (if applic.)	Comments
ERNEST MOERAN (1894—1950) "Blessed Are Those Servants"	SATB & ORG	φ Novello	Anthem 1232	φ CB 8 NAB	Also suitable for Saints Days
JAMES NARES (1715—1783) "Try Me O God"	SATB & ORG	Novello	88001907	—	Also suitable for Lent
CAMILLE SAINT-SAËNS (1835—1921) "Praise Ye The Lord Of Hosts"	SATB & ORG	Belwin Mills	60597	—	From "Christmas Oratorio" (Op. 12)
PETER TCHAIKOVSKY (1840—1893) "Angel Hosts, All Unseen"	SATB*	Basil Ramsey	—	4 Anthems— Tchaikovsky	Some Divisi in all parts. Last two verses suitable for Communion
S. S. WESLEY (1810—1876) "Thou Judge Of Quick and Dead"	SATB & ORG	B & F	—	CAB φ TFB 1961/2	From "Let Us Lift Up Our Heart"
CHARLES WOOD (1866—1926) "O Thou The Central Orb"	SATB & ORG	YBP/ Chappell	A 9	AFC 4	

Composer & Title	Resources	Publisher	Publisher's Reference	Collection in which included (if applic.)	Comments
CHRISTMAS					
RICHARD RODNEY BENNETT (1936—) Five Carols	SATB*	Universal	UE 14010/ 4L	—	Available separately
ANTON BRUCKNER (1824—1896) "Virga Jesse"	SATB*	Peters Annie Bank/ Chester	P-6317 R 12	Peters P-4185	L. only
CHARLES CAMILLERI (1931—) "Christ's Birthday"	SATB*	Roberton	85106	—	
HERBERT HOWELLS (1892—) "Here Is The Little Door"	SATB*	S & B	CCL 216	—	
JOHN JOUBERT (1927—) "There Is No Rose"	SATB*	Novello	—	—	
FRANCIS POULENC (1899—1963) "Hodie Christus Natus Est"	SATB*	Salabert/ U.M.P.	—	—	L. only

CHRISTMAS (Continued)

Composer & Title	Resources	Publisher	Publisher's Reference	Collection in which included (if applic.)	Comments
RICHARD PYGOTT (c.1485–c.1552) "Quid Petis O Fili"	SATB*	S & B	Fayrfax Series 13	—	Macaronic
MAX REGER (1873–1916) "The Virgin's Slumber Song"	SATB & ORG	φ Chappell	—	—	
HEINRICH SCHUTZ (1585–1672) "To Us A Child Is Born"	SATB & ORG	Chappell	1273314	—	E & G
HYLTON STEWART (1884–1932) "On This Day Earth Shall Ring"	SATB & ORG	OUP	A 64	AFC 4 φ TFB 1954	
RALPH VAUGHAN WILLIAMS (1872–1958) "The Blessed Son Of God"	SATB*	OUP	193535270	CFC I	From "Hodie"
PETER WARLOCK (1894–1930) "Bethlehem Down"	SATB*	B & H	—	—	

Composer & Title	Resources	Publisher	Publisher's Reference	Collection in which included (if applic.)	Comments
NEW YEAR'S DAY					
EDWARD C. BAIRSTOW (1874–1946) "Jesu The Very Thought Of Thee"	SATB*	OUP	A 5	∮ CB 7 FSB 7 CAB	Also suitable for Communion
EDWIN EARLE FERGUSON (1910–) "We Pause Beside This Door"	SATB & ORG	Roberton	85020	—	
CHRISTOPHER TYE (c.1500–1573) "Jesu The Very Thought Of Thee"	SATB & ORG (ad lib)	RSCM	FSB 5	—	Also suitable for Communion
HEALEY WILLAN (1880–1968) "Lord Thou Hast Been Our Refuge"	SATB & ORG	BM I/ Universal	—	—	

Composer & Title	Resources	Publisher	Publisher's Reference	Collection in which included (if applic.)	Comments
EPIPHANY					
ADRIAN BATTEN (c.1580–c.1637) "O Praise The Lord"	SATB*	φ OUP	TCM 56	TECM 2 φ TFB 1958 φ CB 9	Coupled with "Deliver Us O Lord Our God" (φ) Also suitable for Missions
JACOB HANDL (1550–1591) "Ab Oriente Venerunt Magi"	SATB*	Müller/ Novello	82151003	—	L. only
C. H. KITSON (Arr) (1874–1944) "Whence Is That Goodly Fragrance"	SATB*	Chappell	076314038	—	
C. S. LANG (1891–1971) "Tres Magi De Gentibus"	SATB & ORG	φ YBP/ Chappell	A 260	FSB 3	
FELIX MENDELSSOHN (1809–1847) "There Shall A Star"	SATB & ORG	φ Novello	Anthem 85	—	Preceded by Optional Treble solo and TBB trio "Say Where Is He Born"

Composer / Title	Voicing	Publisher	Catalogue Nos.	Collection	Notes
F. A. GORE OUSELEY (1825–1889) "From The Rising Of The Sun"	SATB & ORG	RSCM Novello Banks	SB 5 29023003 YS 483	AFC I	
MYRON ROBERTS (1912–) "O Lord We Beseech Thee"	SATB & ORG	H. W. Gray/ Belwin Mills	CMR 2901	—	(Epiphany I). Also suitable for general use
VIRGIL THOMSON (1896–) "The Morning Star"	SATB*	H. W. Gray/ Belwin Mills	GCCS 7	—	Arrangement of Southern U.S.A. traditional hymn tune
CHRISTOPHER TYE (c.1500–1573) "O Come Ye Servants Of The Lord"	SATB*	RSCM Novello Banks	207 29021902 YS 1017	AFC I ∮ FSB 1951	Also suitable for Queen's Accession

Composer & Title	Resources	Publisher	Publisher's Reference	Collection in which included (if applic.)	Comments

SEPTUAGESIMA (See also Evening)

JOSEPH HAYDN (1732–1809)

Composer & Title	Resources	Publisher	Publisher's Reference	Collection in which included (if applic.)	Comments
"Achieved Is The Glorious Work"	SATB & ORG	φ Novello Banks	Choruses 152 — YS 240/330		From "The Creation" (2 Choruses)

Composer & Title	Resources	Publisher	Publisher's Reference	Collection in which included (if applic.)	Comments
SEXAGEISMA					
WILLIAM CROTCH (1775–1847) "How Dear Are Thy Counsels"	SATB*	Novello RSCM	29022910 SB 2	—	Also suitable for Advent II
WILLIAM FOX (? –1579) "Teach Me Thy Way O Lord"	SATB & ORG (ad lib)	Novello φ Chappell	88003204 —	FSB 7	Also suitable for Advent II
GUSTAV HOLST (1874–1934) "Turn Back O Man"	SATB & ORG	S & B	CC 717	TECM 5 AFC 4	
EDMUND HOOPER (c.1553–1621) "Teach Me Thy Way O Lord"	SATB & ORG (ad lib)	OUP	CMS 21a	φ CB 3	Also suitable for Advent II

QUINQUAGESIMA

Composer & Title	Resources	Publisher	Publisher's Reference	Collection in which included (if applic.)	Comments
EDWARD C. BAIRSTOW (1874–1946)					
"Though I Speak With The Tongues Of Men"	SATB & ORG	OUP	A 63	—	Tenor part may be omitted
HENRY LOOSEMORE (? –1670)					
"O Lord Increase Our Faith"	SATB & ORG (ad lib)	RSCM Chester φ Chappell Novello Roberton	FSB 2 — — 29030803 85107	φ CB 5 CAB AECM	Formerly attributed to Orlando Gibbons (Novello)

Composer & Title	Resources	Publisher	Publisher's Reference	Collection in which included (if applic.)	Comments
LENT/PASSIONTIDE					
DOMENICO ALBERTI (1710–1740)					
"O Jesu Salvator"	SATB & ORG	Roberton	85112	—	L & E
FELICE ANERIO (1560–1614)					
"Christus Factus Est"	SATB*	∅Novello	MT 735		L & E
		Chester	—	"Motets Of The Italian School For 4 Voices"	
THOMAS ATTWOOD (1765–1838)					
"Turn Thee Again O Lord"	SATB & ORG	Banks	YS 559	∅ CSB 2	
		Bosworth	—	CAB	
"Turn Thy Face From My Sins"	SATB & ORG	Novello	29022104	TECM 4	Contains Soprano solo
		Banks	YS 248	EA	
				CAB	
ADRIAN BATTEN (c.1580–c.1637)					
"Deliver Us, O Lord Our God"	SATB*	∅ OUP	TCM 56	16c AB	Coupled with "O Praise The Lord"
"Haste Thee O God"	SATB & ORG (ad lib)	OUP	TCM 78	AFC I	

Composer & Title	Resources	Publisher	Publisher's Reference	Collection in which included (if applic.)	Comments
LENT/PASSIONTIDE (Continued)					
GEORGES BIZET (1838–1875)					
"Agnus Dei"	SATB & ORG	Ashdown	305	—	Also suitable for Communion. L & E
JOHN BLOW (1649–1708)					
"Be Merciful Unto Me"	SATB & ORG (ad lib)	OUP	CMS 31	—	
"Let My Prayer Come Up"	SATB & ORG (ad lib)	S & B	MB 7/1	MB 7 TECM AFC I	
WILLIAM BOYCE (1711–1779)					
"Save Me O God"	SATB & ORG	Roberton	85055	—	
ANTON BRUCKNER (1824–1896)					
"Christus Factus Est"	SATB*	Roberton Peters	80887 P-6316	Peters P-4185	L & E L only
		Chappell	1273342		L & E
"Vexilla Regis"	SATB*	Peters	P-6319	Peters P-4185	L only

Composer / Work	Voicing	Publisher	Catalogue	Collection	Notes
WILLIAM BYRD (1543–1623) "Ave Verum Corpus"	SATB*	OUP S & B ϕ Peters ϕ Schott	TCM 3 CC 520 H 1552 —	TECM 2 MHC CAB (English only)	Also suitable for Communion. L & E
JOHN DOWLAND (1563–1626) "Seven Hymn Tunes"	SATB*	OUP	TCM 79/80	—	
EDWARD ELGAR (1857–1934) "Ave Verum Corpus"	SATB & ORG	Novello	30003602	KOG	Also suitable for Communion. L & E
RICHARD FARRANT (? –1581) "Call To Remembrance"	SATB*	OUP Banks	TCM 60 YS 543	CAB	
"Hide Not Thy Face"	SATB*	OUP RSCM	TCM 60 217	TECM 2 CAB ϕ CSB 2	
ORLANDO GIBBONS (1583–1623) "O Lord How Do My Woes Increase"	SATB & ORG (ad lib)	Chester	—	AECM	

LENT/PASSIONTIDE (Continued)

Composer & Title	Resources	Publisher	Publisher's Reference	Collection in which included (if applic.)	Comments
JOHN GOSS (1800–1880) "God So Loved The World"	SATB & ORG	Banks Novello	YS 554 29037401	CAB GSL	Novello edition coupled with "Not Unto Us O Lord" – Walmisley
"O Saviour Of The World"	SATB & ORG (ad lib)	Novello Banks B & F	29023101 YS 403 —	CAB TECM 4 COC	
JOHN HILTON (The Elder) (1560–1608) "Lord For Thy Tender Mercy's Sake"	SATB*	OUP ∅ Novello	CMS 26 Short Anthems 321	EAB CAB COC TECM 2 ∅ CB 6	
JOHN IV OF PORTUGAL (1604–1640) "Crux Fidelis" ⌐ "Faithful Cross" ⌐	SATB*	Bosworth ∅ Cary/ Chappell	— Polyphonic Motets 45	—	Also suitable for Good Friday
KENNETH LEIGHTON (1929—) "Solus Ad Victimam" ("Alone To Sacrifice")	SATB & ORG	OUP	A 309	AFC I	English only

Composer / Work	Voicing	Publisher		Notes
FRANZ LISZT (1811–1886) "O Salutaris Hostia"	SATB*	CUP	—	STS 4 — L & E
HENRY LOOSEMORE (? –1670) "Why Art Thou So Heavy O My Soul"	SATB & ORG (ad lib)	OUP	A 262	—
THOMAS MORLEY (1557–1603) "Nolo Mortem Peccatoris"	SATB & ORG (ad lib)	OUP / Novello	TCM 13 / 29033903	TECM 2 16c AB — Macaronic
W. A. MOZART (1756–1791) "Ave Verum Corpus"	SATB & ORG	Novello / Banks / B & F / φ Schott	29022409 / YS 410 / — / —	EAB / COC / CAB (English L & E only) — Also suitable for Communion. L & E
GEORGE OLDROYD (1886–1951) "Prayer To Jesus"	SATB & ORG	OUP	A 73	—
F. A. GORE OUSELEY (1825–1889) "Is It Nothing To You?"	SATB*	φ Novello	Short Anthems 155	COC / CAB / TECM 4
GIOVANNI PALESTRINA (1525–1594) "We Adore Thee Lord Jesus"	SATB*	φ Novello	—	CAB / GSL

LENT/PASSIONTIDE (Continued)

Composer & Title	Resources	Publisher	Publisher's Reference	Collection in which included (if applic.)	Comments
MARTIN PEERSON (c.1571—c.1650)					
"O God That No Time Dost Despise"	SATB*	Schott	10283	EECM 11	
GIOVANNI PERGOLESI (1710—1736)					
"Miserere Mei"	SATB & ORG	Chappell	1273307	—	L & E
JEAN ROGER-DUCASSE (1873—1954)					
"Crux Fidelis"	SATB & ORG	Durand/UMP	—	—	Contains short Soprano solo. L only
CAMILLE SAINT-SAËNS (1835—1921)					
"Ave Verum Corpus"	SATB*	Roberton Durand/UMP	51521 —		L & E Also suitable for Communion. L only Two different settings
HEINRICH SCHÜTZ (1585—1672)					
"Ponder My Words O Lord"	SATB*	Peters	H-111	—	From "Cantiones Sacrae" (1625)
"Praise To Thee Lord Jesus"	SATB*	Novello	29013900	NAB GSL	

Composer / Title	Voicing	Publisher	No.	Collection	Notes
JOHN SHEPHERD (c.1520–c.1563) "Haste Thee O God"	SATB & ORG (ad lib)	OUP	TCM 77	—	
JOHN STAINER (1840–1901) "God So Loved The World"	SATB*	Novello	29023406	TECM 4	From "The Crucifixion"
C. V. STANFORD (1852–1924) "O For A Closer Walk With God"	SATB & ORG	S & B	CC 703	AFC I ØCB I	Also suitable for Whitsun
THOMAS TALLIS (c.1505–1585) "Purge Me O Lord"	SATB & ORG (ad lib)	OUP	TCM 67	EECM 12	
WILLIAM WALTON (1902–) "A Litany" ("Drop, Drop Slow Tears")	SATB*	OUP	OCS 733	AFC 4	
S. S. WESLEY (1810–1876) "Lead Me Lord"	SATB & ORG	Novello Banks	29030509 YS 510	AFC I EA CAB	Contains short Soprano solo
"Wash Me Throughly"	SATB & ORG	Novello Banks	29011100 YS 681	CAB TECM 4	Contains short Soprano solo

LENT/PASSIONTIDE (Continued)

Composer & Title	Resources	Publisher	Publisher's Reference	Collection in which included (if applic.)	Comments
ARTHUR WILLS (1926—)					
"Ave Verum Corpus"	SATB & ORG	Cramer	—	—	Also suitable for Communion. L & E
MALCOLM WILLIAMSON (1931—)					
"Procession Of Palms"	SATB & ORG	Weinberger	—	—	(Palm Sunday)
HUGO WOLF (1860—1903)					
"Submission"	SATB*	Boonin/ Kalmus Roberton	B 116 51676	—	From 6 Sacred Songs Intensely Chromatic. G & E
NICCOLÒ ZINGARELLI (1752—1837)					
"Christus Factus Est"	SATB*	Roberton	85047	—	L & E
"Haste Thee O God"	SATB & ORG	Banks	YS 433	—	

Composer & Title	Resources	Publisher	Publisher's Reference	Collection in which included (if applic.)	Comments
GOOD FRIDAY					
LUIGI CHERUBINI (1760–1842)					
"Lacrymosa"	SATB & ORG	Roberton	51853	—	From Requiem Mass in C Minor. L & E
MICHAEL HAYDN (1737–1806)					
"Tenebrae Factae Sunt"	SATB*	Boonin/ Kalmus	B 148	—	L & E
"Darkness Was Over The Earth"	SATB & ORG (ad lib)	Peters	P-6377	—	

Composer & Title	Resources	Publisher	Publisher's Reference	Collection in which included (if applic.)	Comments
EASTER					
ANON (c.1600) "This Is The Day"	SATB*	OUP	A 173	16c AB CE	Coupled with "Almighty Lord And God Of Love" – Nathaniel Giles
J. S. BACH (1685–1750) "Awake Thou Wintry Earth"	SATB & ORG	OUP	CMS 16B & 17B	—	Extended Chorale. Difficult accompaniment
"Christians Shout For Joy"	SATB*	RSCM	202	φ CB 3	Chorale
ADRIAN BATTEN (c.1580–1637) "When The Lord Turned Again"	SATB & ORG (ad lib)	OUP	TCM76	16c AB	Coupled with "Lord We Beseech Thee" – Batten
GIOVANNI CROCE (1557–1609) "Virtute Magna"	SATB*	Müller/ Novello	82151809	—	L only
IGNAZIO DONATI (c.1585–1635) "Alleluia, Haec Dies"	SATB & ORG	Faber	—	—	Optional violin part included. L & E

Composer / Title	Scoring	Publisher	No.	Code	Notes
PAUL DRAYTON (1944—)					
"Now Glad Of Heart Be Everyone"	SATB & ORG	Novello	29004106	—	Mostly in Unison
C. ARMSTRONG GIBBS (1889—1960)					
"Most Glorious Lord Of Lyfe"	SATB*	OUP	A 3	CAB	Also entitled "Easter"
JOHN GOSS (1800—1880)					
"If We Believe That Jesus Died"	SATB & ORG	Novello / Banks	29023308 / YS 270	TECM 4 / φCB 6 / CAB	
JOHN IRELAND (1879—1962)					
"Greater Love Hath No Man"	SATB & ORG	S & B	CC 146	AFC 4 / TECM 5	Includes short solos for Soprano and Baritone. Also suitable for Quinquatesima
C. S. LANG (1891—1971)					
"Good Christian Men Rejoice And Sing"	SATB & ORG	RSCM	SB 8	—	
HENRY G. LEY (1887—1962)					
"The Strife Is O'er"	SATB & ORG	OUP	—	φCB 1 / CAB	Based on melody by Melchior Vulpius (1609)
ARTHUR MILNER (1894—)					
"The Lord Is My Shepherd"	SATB & ORG	Lengnick	—	—	(Easter II) Also suitable for Lent IV

EASTER (Continued)

Composer & Title	Resources	Publisher	Publisher's Reference	Collection in which included (if applic.)	Comments
CARL NIELSEN (1865–1931) "Dominus Regit Me"	SATB *	Chester	—	—	From 3 Motets (Op. 55) I only. (Easter II). Also suitable for Lent IV
FRANZ SCHUBERT (1797–1828) "The Lord Is My Shepherd"	SATB & ORG	Novello	29012010	—	(Easter II). Also suitable for Lent IV
HEINRICH SCHÜTZ (1585–1672) "Purge Out The Old Leaven"	SATB & ORG	Peters	P-6593	—	
C. V. STANFORD (1852–1924) "The Lord Is My Shepherd"	SATB & ORG	Novello	29011601	KOG	(Easter II). Also suitable for Lent IV
"Ye Choirs Of New Jerusalem"	SATB & ORG	φ S & B	CC 97	AFC I φ TFB 1954	
S. S. WESLEY (1810–1876) "Blessed Be The God & Father"	SATB & ORG	Novello Banks	29010201 YS 159	CAB TECM 4 φ FSB 1951	Includes Soprano solo
PERCY WHITLOCK (1903–1946) "He Is Risen"	SATB & ORG	φ OUP	E 10	—	

Composer & Title	Resources	Publisher	Publisher's Reference	Collection in which included (if applic.)	Comments
ROGATION					
J. S. BACH (1685–1750) "At Thy Feet In Prayer We Bow"	SATB & ORG	φ S & B	CC 142	φ CSB 3	Contains easy Soprano solo
JOHN MUDD (Fl. 17th Century) "Let Thy Merciful Ears O Lord"	SATB & ORG (ad lib)	OUP φ Schott	TCM 35 —	CAB	Formerly attributed to Thomas Weelkes. Also suitable for Lent
CHARLES WOOD (1866–1926) "O Most Merciful"	SATB & ORG	YBP/ Chappell	076314094	φ CB 9 MHC	Also suitable for Lent/ Passiontide/Good Friday
"Oculi Omnium"	SATB*	YBP/ Chappell	076314094	—	Also suitable for Communion

ASCENSION

Composer & Title	Resources	Publisher	Publisher's Reference	Collection in which included (if applic.)	Comments
J. S. BACH (1685–1750) "Lift Your Heads"	SATB*	RSCM	203	φ CB 4	Chorale type anthem
GIOVANNI CASINI (1670–1715) "Omnes Gentes Plaudite"	SATB*	Müller/Novello	82152109	—	L only
GERALD FINZI (1901–1956) "God Is Gone Up"	SATB & ORG	B & H	CCS 39	TECM 5 φ TFB 1954	Some Divisi in all parts
JACOB HANDL (1550–1591) "Ascendens Christus"	SATB*	Müller/Novello	82152000	—	L only
BRYAN KELLY (1934—) "Rejoice The Lord Is King"	SATB & ORG	Novello	29000401	—	
LUCA MARENZIO (1553–1599) "O Rex Gloriae"	SATB*	OUP	A 303	ED	L only
WILLIAM MATHIAS (1934—) "Lift Up Your Head O Ye Gates"	SATB & ORG	OUP	A 304	AFC I	

Composer / Title	Voicing	Publisher	No.	Publisher	Notes
FELIX MENDELSSOHN (1809–1847) "Above All Praise And Majesty"	SATB & ORG (ad lib)	RSCM / φ Novello	232 / Short Anthems 78	EAB φ FSB 1 Sechs Spruche – Mendelssohn (Chappell)	Version for SSAATTBB published by OUP (A 260) and Chappell. Also suitable for Easter
JOHANN SCHICHT (1753–1823) Ascension Hymn "The Lord Ascendeth Up On High"	SATB & ORG	φ Novello	PCB 1077	NAB	
CHRISTOPHER STEEL (1939–) "O Clap Your Hands Together"	SATB & ORG	Novello	29001507	—	Some Divisi. Ad lib. Brass parts on hire
CHRISTOPHER TYE (c.1500–1573) "Th' Eternal Gates Lift Up Their Heads"	SATB*	RSCM	210	φ CSB 2	Coupled with "How Glorious Sion's Courts Appear" – Tye

WHITSUN

Composer & Title	Resources	Publisher	Publisher's Reference	Collection in which included (if applic.)	Comments
GREGOR AICHINGER (1564—1628) "Confirma Hoc Deus"	SATB*	Chappell	1273299	LD	L & E
THOMAS ATTWOOD (1765—1838) "Come Holy Ghost"	SATB & ORG	Novello Banks	29022300 YS 123	CAB FSB 3 TECM 4	Includes verse for Soprano solo
J. S. BACH (1685—1750) "Awake My Soul And Sing"	SATB*	RSCM	201	GL φ CB 4	Chorale type anthem
MARC-ANTOINE CHARPENTIER (1634—1704) "Come Holy Ghost"	SATB*	CUP	—	STS 4	L & E
CEDRIC THORPE DAVIE (1913— "Come Holy Ghost, The Maker"	SATB & ORG	OUP	A 98	TECM 5	
SYDNEY NICHOLSON (1875—1947) "Love Divine All Love's Excelling"	SATB & ORG	RSCM φ FP	212 —	GL φ SNCB	Also suitable for Quinquagesima

Composer / Title	Voicing	Publisher	Catalogue	Collection	Notes
THOMAS TALLIS (c.1505–1585)					
"If Ye Love Me"	SATB & ORG (ad lib)	OUP Banks Novello Peters	TCM 69 YS 834 29022703 H-1476	TECM 2 FSB 6 CAB EECM 12	
"O Lord Give Thy Holy Spirit"	SATB & ORG (ad lib)	OUP φ Chappell	TCM 68 ——	GL 16c AB EECM 12	
CHRISTOPHER TYE (c.1500–1573)					
"O Holy Spirit, Lord Of Grace"	SATB*	RSCM	209	GL φ CSB 1	Also suitable for Confirmation
TOMÁS LUIS DE VICTORIA (1549–1611)					
"Beati Immaculati"	SATB*	Chappell	1273296	ED	L & E
ALFRED WHITEHEAD (1887–1974)					
"Come Holy Ghost In Love"	SATB*	Harris/Lengnick	HC 4008	——	

TRINITY SUNDAY

Composer & Title	Resources	Publisher	Publisher's Reference	Collection in which included (if applic.)	Comments
WILLIAM BOYCE (1711–1779) "Blessing And Glory"	SATB & ORG	Roberton	85054	—	Includes some simple Divisi
ANDREA GABRIELI (c.1510–1586) "Te Deum Patrem"	SATB*	Müller/Novello	82152305	—	L only
ALUN HODDINOTT (1929–) "Holy, Holy, Holy"	SATB*	OUP	A 210	—	
FRANZ SCHUBERT (1797–1828) "Zum Sanctus"	SATB & ORG	Roberton	85048	—	L & E
HEINRICH SCHÜTZ (1585–1672) "Praise And Thanks To God"	SATB*	Chappell	1273279	—	E & G
PETER TCHAIKOVSKY (1840–1893) "Blessed Angel Spirits"	SATB*	Novello	29023602	CAB	("Hymn To The Trinity")
"Cherubic Hymn"	SATB*	Banks	YS 142	—	
CHARLES WOOD (1866–1926) "God Omnipotent Reigneth"	SATB & ORG	⌀YBP/Chappell	A 50	FSB 6	

Composer & Title	Resources	Publisher	Publisher's Reference	Collection in which included (if applic.)	Comments
SAINTS DAYS					
EDGAR BAINTON (1880–1956) "And I Saw A New Heaven"	SATB & ORG	Novello	29034203	TECM 5 FSB 4	(All Saints)
ERNEST BULLOCK (1890–) "Give Us The Wings Of Faith"	SATB & ORG	OUP	A 1	AFC 4 ∅ SNCB	
MAURICE DURUFLÉ (1902–) "Tu Es Petrus"	SATB*	Durand/ UMP	—	—	(St Peter) L only
GABRIEL FAURÉ (1845–1924) "Tu Es Petrus"	SATB & ORG	Durand/ UMP	—	—	(St Peter) Contains simple Baritone solo
MICHAEL FRITH (1941–) "Bless The Lord All His Angels"	SATB & ORG	RSCM	FSB 7	—	
ANDREA GABRIELI (c.1510–1586) "Angeli, Archangeli"	SATB*	Müller/ Novello	82154103	—	L only

Composer & Title	Resources	Publisher	Publisher's Reference	Collection in which included (if applic.)	Comments
SAINTS DAYS (Continued)					
ALAN GRAY (1855–1935)					
"What Are These That Glow From Afar"	SATB & ORG	φ S & B	CC 325	—	(All Saints)
WILLIAM HARRIS (1883–1973)					
"Holy Is The True Light"	SATB*	φ Novello	MT 1259	FSB 7	
HERBERT HOWELLS (1892–)					
"A Hymn For St Cecilia"	SATB & ORG	φ Novello	MT 1426	—	Contains much unison writing
HENRY G. LEY (1887–1962)					
"Lo Round The Throne A Glorious Band"	SATB & ORG	OUP	—	CAB FSB 3	Based on a melody by N. Herman (1560)
LUCA MARENZIO (1553–1599)					
"O Quam Gloriosum"	SATB*	Müller/Novello	82154310	—	(All Saints) L only
FELIX MENDELSSOHN (1809–1847)					
"How Lovely Are The Messengers"	SATB & ORG	Banks	YS 226	—	(Evangelists)

Composer / Title	Voicing	Publisher	No.	Ref.	Notes
JOHN STAINER (1840–1901) "How Beautiful Upon The Mountains"	SATB & ORG	Novello	29031408	SEA I ⌀ CB 8 TECM 4	(Evangelists)
C. V. STANFORD (1852–1924) "And I Saw Another Angel"	SATB & ORG	⌀ Novello	Short Anthems 20	—	(St Michael & All Angels, All Saints) Contains short Tenor solo
"How Beauteous Are Their Feet"	SATB & ORG	Novello	29024000	⌀ CB 3 NAB	(Evangelists)
PETER TCHAIKOVSKY (1840–1893) "How Blessed Are They"	SATB*	Basil Ramsey	—	4 Anthems — Tchaikovsky	Contains considerable straightforward Divisi
CHRISTOPHER TYE (c.1500–1573) "Hail Glorious Spirits, Heirs Of Light"	SATB*	RSCM	221	⌀ CB 10	
TOMÁS LUIS DE VICTORIA (1549–1611) "O Quam Gloriosum"	SATB*	Novello ⌀ Chappell	29013704	—	(All Saints) L & E

BLESSED VIRGIN MARY

Composer & Title	Resources	Publisher	Publisher's Reference	Collection in which included (if applic.)	Comments
ALLESSANDRO GRANDI (? –1630) "O Porta Caeli"	SATB & ORG	Novello	29026310	—	L & E
FRANZ LISZT (1811–1886) "Salve Regina"	SATB*	Roberton	85056	—	L & E
FRANCIS POULENC (1899–1963) "Salve Regina"	SATB*	Salabert/ UMP	—	—	L only
JEAN ROGER-DUCASSE (1873–1954) "Alma Redemptoris Mater"	SATB & ORG	Durand/ UMP	—	—	Contains short Soprano solo. L only
"Regina Coeli Laetare"	SATB & ORG	Durand/ UMP	—	—	L only
GIOACCHINO ROSSINI (1792–1868) "Ave Maria"	SATB & ORG	Roberton	85051	—	L & E
CAMILLE SAINT-SAËNS (1835–1921) "Ave Maria"	SATB & ORG	Durand/ UMP	—	—	L only

FLORENT SCHMITT (1870–1958) "Ave Regina Coelorum"	SATB & ORG	Durand/UMP	—	—	L only
IGOR STRAVINSKY (1882–1971) "Ave Maria"	SATB*	B & H	CCS 28	—	L only
PETER TCHAIKOVSKY (1840–1893) "In Truth It Is Meet"	SATB*	Basil Ramsey	—	4 Anthems – Tchaikovsky	Some Divisi in Bass part. (Published as "Why Is My Heart With Grief Oppressed" By Chappell (1273316)
LOUIS VIERNE (1870–1937) "Ave Maria"	SATB & ORG	Hamelle/UMP	—	—	L only
PIERRE VILLETTE (1926—) "Hymne À La Vierge"	SATB*	Durand/UMP	—	—	Some Divisi. Very effective. Written in 1954. F only

Composer & Title	Resources	Publisher	Publisher's Reference	Collection in which included (if applic.)	Comments
DEDICATION					
JOHANNES BRAHMS (1833–1897)					
"How Lovely Are Thy Dwellings" "How Pleasant Are Thy Dwellings" "How Lovely Is Thy Dwelling Place"	SATB & ORG	Novello Banks Peters	29013007 YS 623 P-3672B	CAB	From "German Requiem"
ANTON BRUCKNER (1824–1896)					
"Locus Iste"	SATB*	Peters	P-6314	Peters P-4185 STS 4	L only
		∅ Schott	—		L & G
JOHN GOSS (1800–1880)					
"O Pray For The Peace Of Jerusalem"	SATB & ORG	∅ Novello	—	AFC I ∅ CSB I ∅ CB 2	
WILLIAM HARRIS (1883–1973)					
"Behold The Tabernacle Of God"	SATB & ORG	RSCM	208	—	
HERBERT HOWELLS (1892–)					
"O Pray For The Peace Of Jerusalem"	SATB & ORG	OUP	A 107	—	

ROY SLACK (1912–)					
"I Was Glad"	SATB & ORG	OUP	E 105	—	
C. V. STANFORD (1852–1924)					
"Glorious And Powerful God"	SATB*	φ S & B	CC 166	—	
CHRISTOPHER TYE (c.1500–1573)					
"How Glorious Sion's Courts Appear"	SATB*	RSCM	210	φ CSB 2	Coupled with "Th' Eternal Gates Lift Up Their Heads" — Tye
RALPH VAUGHAN WILLIAMS (1872–1958)					
"O How Amiable Are Thy Dwellings"	SATB & ORG	OUP	A 94	AFC 4 EAB	
CHARLES WOOD (1866–1926)					
"Glorious And Powerful God"	SATB & ORG	φ Novello	—	φ CSB 2	

MISSIONS

Composer & Title	Resources	Publisher	Publisher's Reference	Collection in which included (if applic.)	Comments
JOHN TRAVERS (c.1703–1758) "O Worship The Lord"	SATB & ORG	Novello	29010909	TECM 3 φ CB 5 φ TFB 1951	From "Ascribe Unto The Lord"
RALPH VAUGHAN WILLIAMS (1872–1958) "Let All The World"	SATB & ORG	φ S & B	CC 349	FSB 8	Also suitable for Thanksgiving. Difficult organ part
S. S. WESLEY (1810–1876) "The Lord Hath Been Mindful Of Us"	SATB & ORG	Novello	29011805	φ TFB 1958	From "Ascribe Unto The Lord"

Composer & Title	Resources	Publisher	Publisher's Reference	Collection in which included (if applic.)	Comments
MORNING					
HAROLD DARKE (1888–1976)					
"Christ Whose Glory Fills The Skies"	SATB & ORG	RSCM	—	FSB 2	
THOMAS FORD (1580–1648)					
"Almighty God Which Hast Me Brought"	SATB & ORG (ad lib)	RSCM	230	CAB	
		OUP	A 183	SEA I	
		Banks	YS 1517	φFSB I	
		Novello	29030705	AFC I	
		Peters	H-1558	EECM 11	

Composer & Title	Resources	Publisher	Publisher's Reference	Collection in which included (if applic.)	Comments
EVENING					
ANON (16th Century) "O Lord, The Maker Of All Thing"	SATB*	OUP	TCM 83	16c AB	Also suitable for Septuagesima
J. S. BACH (1685–1750) "Jesus Is The Loveliest Light"	SATB & ORG (ad lib)	Roberton	85053	—	Chorale
EDWARD C. BAIRSTOW (1874–1946) "Save Us O Lord, Waking"	SATB & ORG	Novello	29012105	—	
WILLIAM BLITHEMAN (? –1591) "In Pace"	SATB*	Novello	29025400	—	L & E
HAROLD DARKE (1888–1976) "O Gladsome Light"	SATB & ORG	φ OUP	A 31	—	
H. BALFOUR GARDINER (1877–1950) "Evening Hymn" ("Te Lucis Ante Terminum")	SATB & ORG	Novello	29013301	KOG	L & E

JOHN JOUBERT (1927–) "O Lorde The Maker Of Al Thing"	SATB & ORG	Novello	29025008	KOG φ FSB 1961/2	Also suitable for Septuagesima
WILLIAM MUNDY (c.1529–1591) "O Lord The Maker Of All Things"	SATB*	OUP	TCM 38	CAB TECM 2	Also suitable for Septuagesima
TOMAS DE SANTA MARIÁ (? – ? 1570) "All Holy Lord"	SATB*	φ Novello	MT 1434	—	
GEOFFREY SHAW (1879–1943) "Hail Gladdening Light"	SATB & ORG	φ Novello RSCM	MT 895 SB 7	SEA I NAB	

Composer & Title	Resources	Publisher	Publisher's Reference	Collection in which included (if applic.)	Comments
COMMUNION					
GREGOR AICHINGER (1564—1628)					
"Adoramus Te"	SATB*	Chappell	1273290	—	L & E
ANTON BRUCKNER (1824—1896)					
"Pange Lingua"	SATB*	Peters	P-6313	Peters P-4185	L only
WILLIAM BYRD (1543—1623)					
"Sacerdotes Domini"	SATB*	OUP S & B	TCM 4 CC 415	16c AB MHC	L & E Also suitable for Epiphany
GIOVANNI CROCE (1560—1609)					
"We Taste Thee O Thou Living Bread"	SATB*	Banks	YS 1157	—	E only
MAURICE DURUFLÉ (1902—)					
"Tantum Ergo"	SATB*	Durand/ UMP	—	—	L only
CÉSAR FRANCK (1822—1890)					
"Panis Angelicus"	SATB & ORG	Ashdown	131	—	L & E
G. F. HANDEL (1685—1759)					
"Lord I Trust Thee"	SATB & ORG	RSCM	FSB 7	AFC I	

Composer / Title	Voicing	Publisher	Cat. No.	Series	Notes
WILLIAM HARRIS (1883–1973) "The Holy Eucharist"	SATB*	OUP	A 233	—	
RICHARD LLOYD (1933–) "View Me Lord"	SATB*	Novello	29031506	SEA 2	
OLIVIER MESSIAEN (1908–) "O Sacrum Convivium"	SATB & ORG (ad lib)	Durand/ UMP	—	—	Difficult
GIOVANNI PERGOLESI (1710–1736) "O Sacrum Convivium"	SATB & ORG (ad lib)	Chappell	1273270	—	L & E
GIUSEPPE PITONI (1657–1743) "In Voce Exsultationis"	SATB*	Müller/	82153008	—	L only
"Tantum Ergo"	SATB*	Novello	82174901	—	L only
CAMILLE SAINT-SAËNS (1835–1921) "Panis Angelicus"	SATB & ORG	Durand/ UMP	—	—	
THOMAS TALLIS (c.1505–1585) "Verily, Verily I Say Unto You"	SATB & ORG	OUP	A 247	EECM 12 AFC I	Also suitable for Passiontide

Composer & Title	Resources	Publisher	Publisher's Reference	Collection in which included (if applic.)	Comments
COMMUNION (Continued)					
RALPH VAUGHAN WILLIAMS (1872–1958)					
"O Taste And See"	SATB & ORG	OUP	—	TECM 5 AFC 4 EAB	Includes Soprano solo
TOMÁS LUIS DE VICTORIA (1549–1611)					
"Jesu The Very Thought Of Thee" ("Jesus Dulcis Memoria")	SATB & ORG (ad lib)	OUP	CMS 8B	MHC EAB CAB	Also suitable for Passiontide
LOUIS VIERNE (1870–1937)					
"Tantum Ergo"	SATB & ORG	Noël/ UMP	—	—	L only
PERCY WHITLOCK (1903–1946)					
"Here O My Lord, I See Thee Face To Face"	SATB & ORG	OUP	A 42	MHC	Some Divisi
CHARLES WOOD (Arr) (1866–1926)					
"Jesu The Very Thought Is Sweet"	SATB*	F.P.	—	φ FSB 1951 CAB	Melody from Piae Cantiones. Also suitable for New Years' Day

Composer & Title	Resources	Publisher	Publisher's Reference	Collection in which included (if applic.)	Comments
REMEMBRANCE					
PETER ASTON (1938–) "So They Gave Their Bodies"	SATB & ORG	RSCM	—	FSB 8	
ALAN GRAY (1855–1935) "The Dead" ("Blow Out Ye Bugles")	SATB & ORG	φ S & B	—	—	
KIEFF MELODY (Arr Walter Parratt) "Give Rest O Christ"	SATB*	φ Novello	50011405	—	
LEO SOWERBY (1895–1968) "Let Us Now Praise Famous Men"	SATB & ORG	RSCM	223	φ CB 10	

FUNERALS/MEMORIALS

Composer & Title	Resources	Publisher	Publisher's Reference	Collection in which included (if applic.)	Comments
WILLIAM CHILD (1606–1697) "I Heard A Voice From Heaven"	SATB*	φ Chappell	—	—	
THOMAS MORLEY (1557–1603) "Thou Knowest Lord"	SATB*	φ Chappell	—	—	Also suitable for Lent
HENRY PURCELL (1659–1695) "Thou Knowest Lord"	SATB & ORG	Novello B & F	29014908 —	CAB TECM 3 φ FSB 1951	Also suitable for Lent

WEDDINGS

Composer & Title	Resources	Publisher	Publisher's Reference	Collection in which included (if applic.)	Comments
EDWARD C. BAIRSTOW (1874–1946)					
"I Sat Down Under His Shadow"	SATB*	OUP	A 4	AFC I	Also suitable for Communion
PATRICK HADLEY (1899–1973)					
"My Beloved Spake"	SATB & ORG	Curwen	61345	—	Also suitable for Easter
WILLIAM HARRIS (1883–1973)					
"The Lord My Pasture Shall Prepare"	SATB & ORG	Novello	29034802	NAB	Also suitable for Lent

HARVEST

Composer & Title	Resources	Publisher	Publisher's Reference	Collection in which included (if applic.)	Comments
LEONARD BLAKE (1907–) "Sing To The Lord Of Harvest"	SATB & ORG	RSCM	215	φ CSB 2	
MAURICE GREENE (1695–1755) "Thou Visitest The Earth"	SATB & ORG SAB & ORG	Novello Banks —	88001308 YS 166 —	φ CB 1 CAB HFM	Also suitable for Rogationtide
WILLIAM HARRIS (1883–1973) "Fear Not O Land"	SATB & ORG	OUP	E 73	—	
"Glory, Love And Praise And Honour"	SATB & ORG	RSCM	236	HFM	Melody by Johann Eberlin
CHARLES MACPHERSON (1870–1927) "Thou O God Art Praised In Sion"	SATB & ORG	φ Novello	MT 932	φ CB 9	
SYDNEY NICHOLSON (1875–1947) "Let Us With A Gladsome Mind"	SATB & ORG	RSCM	243	SB 1	
CHARLES WOOD (1866–1926) "Summer Ended"	SATB & ORG	φ YBP/ Chappell	—	HFM	

Composer & Title	Resources	Publisher	Publisher's Reference	Collection in which included (if applic.)	Comments
ORDINATIONS					
JOHN BLOW (1649–1708)					
"Let Thy Hand Be Strengthened"	SATB & ORG	φ Novello Schott	Anthem 1097 10293	SEA 2	Also suitable for the Queen's Accession

GENERAL & THANKSGIVING

Composer & Title	Resources	Publisher	Publisher's Reference	Collection in which included (if applic.)	Comments
PETER ASTON (1938—)					
"For I Went With The Multitude"	SATB & ORG	Novello	29001202	—	
EMMANUELE D'ASTORGA (1681—1736)					
"Oh What Sorrow"	SATB & ORG	Roberton	85065	—	Also suitable for Lent & Easter
J. S. BACH (1685—1750)					
"Awake Us Lord And Hasten"	SATB & ORG	RSCM	231	φ FSB I AFC I	Extended Chorale. Printed in CAB as "Subdue Us By Thy Goodness"
"God Is Living, God Is Here"	SATB & ORG (ad lib)	OUP	E 112	AFC I	Chorale type anthem
"Jesu Joy Of Man's Desiring"	SATB & ORG	OUP	CMS 16A	CAB	Extended Chorale
GEORGE BARCROFTE (Fl. c.1600)					
"O Lord We Beseech Thee"	SATB & ORG (ad lib)	OUP	A 256	—	Coupled with "O Almighty God" — Barcrofte Epiphany II (AFC I)

Composer / Title	Voicing	Publisher	Number	Collection	Notes
ADRIAN BATTEN (c.1580–c.1637) "O Sing Joyfully" ⎱ "Sing We Merrily" ⎰	SATB*	OUP RSCM Novello ⌀ Peters	A 190 228 29012402 H-1551	16c AB ⌀ CB 7	
JEAN BERGER (1909–) "O Give Thanks Unto The Lord"	SATB*	Kalmus	5366	—	Some Divisi in S & T
JOHN BLOW (1649–1708) "O Pray For The Peace Of Jerusalem"	SATB & ORG	Novello	29014505	FSB 2	Optional Soprano solo. Also suitable for Dedication
JOHANNES BRAHMS (1833–1897) "Alas Poor World"	SATB*	Peters	P-6645	—	E & G
"O Saviour Rend The Heavens"	SATB*	Peters	P-6560	—	E & G
BENJAMIN BRITTEN (1913–1976) "O Be Joyful In The Lord" (Jubilate Deo)	SATB & ORG	OUP	S 551	AFC 4	
WILLIAM BYRD (1543–1623) "Prevent Us O Lord In All Our Doings"	SATB*	OUP	CMS 13B	⌀ TFB 1961/2	

Composer & Title	Resources	Publisher	Publisher's Reference	Collection in which included (if applic.)	Comments
GENERAL & THANKSGIVING (Continued)					
SYDNEY CAMPBELL (1909–1974)					
"Be Strong And Of Good Courage"	SATB & ORG	φ Novello	MT 1394	FSB 7	
"Praise To God In The Highest"	SATB & ORG	OUP	—	φ CB 9 AFC I	Arranged from OBC 107
"Sing We Merrily Unto God"	SATB & ORG	Novello	29025302	—	
E. T. CHAPMAN (1902–)					
"Let All The World In Every Corner Sing"	SATB & ORG	φ Chappell	—	—	Also suitable for Missions
WILLIAM CROTCH (1775–1847)					
"Comfort O Lord"	SATB & ORG	Banks	YS 472	φ CSB I SEA I CAB	Also suitable for Lent
		Novello	29022910		
CÉSAR FRANCK (1822–1890)					
"Psalm 150"	SATB & ORG	Novello	29014309	—	L only
		Durand/ UMP	—		L only
		Belwin Mills	64008		E only

	Voicing	Publisher	Number	Series	Notes
MELCHIOR FRANCK (c.1573—1639)					
"Jesus, Thy Cross Redeem My Soul"					
"When Fears Of Death"	SATB*	Peters	P-66033	—	
MICHAEL FRITH (1941—)					
"Let The People Praise Thee O God"	SATB & ORG	RSCM	—	FSB 8	
ORLANDO GIBBONS (1583—1625)					
"Almighty & Everlasting God"	SATB & ORG (ad lib)	OUP	TCM 36	φCB 8 CAB	Also suitable for Epiphany III and Hospital Sunday
"Deliver Us O Lord Our God"	SATB*	Chappell	1273300	—	—
NATHANIEL GILES (c.1560—1633)					
"Almighty Lord And God Of Love"	SATB & ORG (ad lib)	OUP	A 173	EECM 11	Coupled with "This Is The Day" — Anon
ALEXANDER GOEHR (1932—)					
"The Man Of Life" (Virtutes 2B)	SATB*	Schott	10860	—	
"O Gracious God" (Virtutes 5)	SATB & ORG	Schott	10863	—	
JOHN GOSS (1800—1880)					
"Almighty And Merciful God"	SATB*	φNovello	40020008	φCB 9	(Trinity III)

Composer & Title	Resources	Publisher	Publisher's Reference	Collection in which included (if applic.)	Comments
GENERAL & THANKSGIVING (Continued)					
EDVARD GRIEG (1843–1907)					
"O Father Of Life" (Op. 74 No. 1)	SATB*	Roberton	51581	4 Psalms (Op. 74) (Peters P-3128A)	Divisi in Soprano part. Contains easy Baritone solo
G. F. HANDEL (1685–1759)					
"Let Their Celestial Concerts"	SATB & ORG	Banks Novello	YS 310 29020709	— —	From "Samson"
"O Father Whose Almighty Power"	SATB & ORG	Banks	YS 211	—	
"The King Shall Rejoice"	SATB & ORG	RSCM	—	FSB 8	
"With Cheerful Notes"	SATB & ORG	ɸ Novello	Anthem 1188	ɸ CB 4	From 6th Chandos Anthem
		ɸ Schott	—	ɸ TFB 1961/2	
WILLIAM HARRIS (1883–1973)					
"All Creatures Of Our God And King"	SATB*	RSCM	222	ɸ CB 10	Also suitable for Septuagesima
"Prevent Us O Lord"	SATB*	Novello	29027209	—	Tonic Solfa included

JOSEPH HAYDN (1732–1809)

Title	Voicing	Publisher	No.		Notes
"Insanae Et Vanae Curae"	SATB & ORG	∅ Novello	Choruses 359	—	L only
"Lord We Pray Thee"	SATB & ORG	Banks	YS 505	—	(Trinity XVII)

HERBERT HOWELLS (1892–)

Title	Voicing	Publisher	No.		Notes
"Like As The Hart"	SATB & ORG	OUP	A 109	AFC 4	
"My Eyes For Beauty Pine"	SATB & ORG	OUP	A 14	EAB	Mostly in Unison
"Thee Will I Love"	SATB & ORG	Novello	29015502	—	Simple Divisi on last page

JOHN JOUBERT (1927–)

Title	Voicing	Publisher	No.		Notes
"How Are My Foes Increased Lord"	SATB & ORG	Novello	86002905	—	

JOHANN KRIEGER (1649–1725)

Title	Voicing	Publisher	No.		Notes
"For The Righteous Shall Be Swept Away From Misfortune"	SATB & ORG	Roberton	80898	—	

JEAN LANGLAIS (1907–)

Title	Voicing	Publisher	No.		Notes
"Festival Alleluia"	SATB & ORG	Elkan-Vogel/UMP	—	—	Some Divisi

ORLANDUS LASSUS (Orlando Di Lasso) (1532–1594)

Title	Voicing	Publisher	No.		Notes
"Dextera Domini"	SATB*	Chappell	1273301	—	L & E
"Jubilate Deo, Omnis Terra"	SATB*	Peters	P-4882	MFS	Coupled with "Sicut Cervus" – Palestrina L & G

Composer & Title	Resources	Publisher	Publisher's Reference	Collection in which included (if applic.)	Comments
GENERAL & THANKSGIVING (Continued)					
KENNETH LEIGHTON (1929–)					
"O God Enfold Me In The Sun"	SATB & ORG	OUP	A 246	—	Also suitable for Saints Days
STANLEY MARCHANT (1883–1949)					
"Judge Eternal"	SATB & ORG	Novello	29014004	ø CSB 4 NAB	(National). Also suitable for Advent
WILLIAM MATHIAS (1934–)					
"Bless The Lord O My Soul"	SATB & ORG	OUP	A 284	—	Also suitable for Septuagesima
"The Law Of The Lord"	SATB*	OUP	A 301	—	
"Make A Joyful Noise Unto The Lord"	SATB & ORG	OUP	A 220	FSB 5 AFC 4	
FELIX MENDELSSOHN (1809–1847)					
"He That Shall Endure To The End"	SATB & ORG	Banks	YS 322	—	

	Voicing	Publisher	No.		Notes
W. A. MOZART (1756–1791) "Laudate Pueri"	SATB & ORG	Roberton	80900	—	From "Vesperae Solennes De Confessore" (K. 339) L & E
"O God When Thou Appearest" ("Splendente Te Deus")	SATB & ORG	Banks	YS 783	—	Duets may be sung full. Difficult organ part. English only. Also suitable for Septuagesima and Ascension
JOHN MUDD (Fl. 17th Century) "God Which Hast Prepared"	SATB & ORG (ad lib)	OUP RSCM	A 212 235	φ CSB 5	
VINCENT NOVELLO (1781–1861) "Like As The Hart"	SATB & ORG	Banks RSCM φ Novello	YS 434 SB 9 Short Anthems 219	—	
GIOVANNI PALESTRINA (1525–1594) "Sicut Cervus"	SATB*	Peters	P-4882	—	Coupled with "Jubilate Deo" – Lassus. L & G

Composer & Title	Resources	Publisher	Publisher's Reference	Collection in which included (if applic.)	Comments
GENERAL & THANKSGIVING (Continued)					
C. H. H. PARRY (1848–1918)					
"My Soul There Is A Country"	SATB*	Chappell	—	TECM 5 CAB	One of the "Songs of Farewell"
"Prevent Us O Lord"	SATB & ORG (ad lib)	OUP	CMS 27	—	
GIUSEPPE PITONI (1657–1743)					
"Cantate Domino" / "Sons Of Jerusalem"	SATB*	ø Cary/ Chappell RSCM	Polyphonic Motets 24 SB 10	AFC I	L & E
"Laudate Dominum"	SATB*	ø Cary/ Chappell	Westminster Series 4	LD	L only
BERNARD ROSE (1916–)					
"Behold I Make All Things New"	SATB & ORG	Roberton	85049	—	
MICHAEL ROSE (1934–)					
"Sing To The Lord A Joyful Song"	SATB & ORG	øOUP	E 113	—	
ALEC ROWLEY (1892–1958)					
"Praise"	SATB & ORG	OUP	A 24	—	

Composer / Title	Voicing	Publisher			Notes
EDMUND RUBBRA (1901–)					
"Prayer To Jesus"	SATB & ORG (ad lib)	Lengnick		—	Both in same leaflet
"That Virgin's Child"					
JOHN RUTTER (1945–)					
"God Be In My Head"	SATB*	OUP	—	FSB 7	
"Praise Ye The Lord"	SATB & ORG	OUP	E 120	AFC-1	
ALESSANDRO SCARLATTI (1660–1725)					
"Exsultate Deo"	SATB*	Annie Bank/ Chester	B 10	—	Published by RSCM (252) as "Sing Aloud With Gladness" L only
FLORENT SCHMITT (1870–1958)					
"Laudate Dominum"	SATB & ORG	Durand/ UMP	—	—	L only
HEATHCOTE STATHAM (1889–1973)					
"Praise Thou The Lord"	SATB & ORG	φ Novello	MT 1345	KOG	
CHRISTOPHER STEEL (1939–)					
"Thou Art The Way"	SATB & ORG	Novello	MW 3	—	Opening Baritone solo may be sung full
JAN SWEELINCK (1562–1621)					
"Psalm 90"	SATB*	Mercury/ Kalmus	MC 3	—	F & E

GENERAL & THANKSGIVING (Continued)

Composer & Title	Resources	Publisher	Publisher's Reference	Collection in which included (if applic.)	Comments
CHRISTOPHER TYE (c.1500–1573)					
"Praise Ye The Lord, Ye Children"	SATB & ORG (ad lib)	OUP	TCM 58	—	
ORAZIO VECCHI (1550–1605)					
"Cantate Domino"	SATB & ORG (ad lib)	Roberton	85005	—	L & E
ANTONIO VIVALDI (1678–1741)					
"Laetatus Sum" (Psalm 122)	SATB & ORG	Roberton	51670	—	Also suitable for Dedication. L & E
GEORG GOTTFRIED WAGNER (1698–1759)					
"Blessing, Glory And Thanks"	SATB*	Roberton φ Novello	51179 OC 661	—	Also suitable for Trinity Sunday
THOMAS ATTWOOD WALMISLEY (1814–1856)					
"From All That Dwell"	SATB & ORG (ad lib)	RSCM	216	CAB φ CSB 3	Also suitable for Missions
"Not Unto Us O Lord"	SATB & ORG	Banks Novello	YS 435 29037401	AFC I	Novello edition coupled with "God So Loved The World" – Goss

	Voicing	Publisher	CMS 20c	EECM 11	Notes
JOHN WARD (1571–1638)					
"O Let Me Tread In The Right Path"	SATB*	OUP	CMS 20c	EECM 11	Also suitable for Sexegesima
S. S. WESLEY (1810–1876)					
"O Lord My God"	SATB & ORG	Banks / RSCM / φ Novello	YS 167 / FSB 8 / MT 314	CAB	Also suitable for Dedication & Lent
"Thou Wilt Keep Him In Perfect Peace"	SATB & ORG	Novello / Banks	29015208 / YS 1536	TECM 4 / SEA 2 / CAB	Original SATTB version available – Banks (YS 699) & Novello (29010408)
ARTHUR WILLS (1926–)					
"Behold Now Praise The Lord"	SATB & ORG	RSCM	234	φ CSB 5	
HUGO WOLF (1860–1903)					
"Exaltation"	SATB*	Roberton / Boonin / Kalmus / φ Schott	51677 / B 117 / —	—	From 6 Sacred Songs – both intensely chromatic
"Looking Upwards"	SATB*	Roberton / Boonin / Kalmus / φ Schott	51672 / B 112 / —	—	E & G
CHARLES WOOD (1866–1926)					
"Expectans Expectavi"	SATB & ORG	YBP/	076314244	—	English words
"O Thou Sweetest Source"	SATB & ORG	Chappell	076314276	φ CB 6	——